The Banality of Grace

The Banality of Grace

By
BRUCE K. MODAHL

Foreword by
JILL PELÁEZ BAUMGAERTNER

CASCADE *Books* • Eugene, Oregon

THE BANALITY OF GRACE

Cascade Books
An Imprint of Wipf and Stock Publishers
199 W. 8th Ave., Suite 3
Eugene, OR 97401

www.wipfandstock.com

PAPERBACK ISBN: 978-1-5326-6037-5
HARDCOVER ISBN: 978-1-5326-6038-2
EBOOK ISBN: 978-1-5326-6039-9

Cataloguing-in-Publication data:

Names: Modahl, Bruce K., author. | Baumgaertner, Jill Peláez, foreword.

Title: The banality of grace / Bruce K. Modahl ; foreword by Jill Peláez Baumgaertner.

Description: Eugene, OR : Cascade Books, 2019 | Includes bibliographical references.

Identifiers: ISBN 978-1-5326-6037-5 (paperback) | ISBN 978-1-5326-6038-2 (hardcover) | ISBN 978-1-5326-6039-9 (ebook)

Subjects: LCSH: Grace (Theology).

Classification: BT761.3 .M63 2019 (paperback) | BT761.3 .M63 (ebook)

Manufactured in the U.S.A.   06/18/19

Contents

Permissions

Foreword

Grace doesn't make sense. And that is precisely the point. As the parable teaches, those who work hard in twelve-hour shifts, harvesting, gathering, tying sheaves of wheat into bundles and hauling to wagons, or watering and yoking the oxen, driving them to barns, receive the same wages as those who are hired for the last hour of the day, lugging only a partial wagonload of wheat into the barn. Roofers working in the July sun, bakers waiting in the predawn hours as the dough rises, attorneys preparing briefs, and teachers grading papers; whatever profession you are in, just think about this: when it comes to your salvation, it doesn't matter how hard you have worked or the level of excellence you have achieved through that hard work. Grace is like a PhD given to a person who never took an exam or wrote a dissertation—but signed up for only one class. Grace is not fair, and for that reason we find it difficult to understand, but as Luther writes, "Really, we ought to spit on ourselves and become angry with ourselves for being such wretched folk that we insist on justice instead of the grace which is offered."

Grace not only makes no sense, it can be downright terrifying. It defies everything the world has taught us, and there is absolutely nothing we can do except hold out our hands to receive it or turn our backs on it. For this reason, grace is an ominous freedom. It is offered and we can only step forward into the unknown. "But," Luther writes, "grace steps out cheerfully into the darkness, follows the bare Word and Scripture, no matter what matters appear to be like; whether human nature thinks them to be right or wrong, grace clings to the Word."

I have tried to write about grace in several poems over the past few years. I have attempted to pin it down, to make it make sense. In one, I compared grace to the transparency and lift of air, or the freedom of the pebble flinging out of the slingshot, or the usually tethered dog suddenly free of the leash. I imagined myself on a dark beach at midnight, the surf loud, the horizon invisible, the entire world the threat of rushing water. Swimming at night in the ocean is daunting, one's sense of direction sometimes unclear. At the end of the poem I ask: "Swimming: / is it toward the shore lights / or is it out into the vast bed / of the sea's white fires?" Grace should be a comforting concept, and for many it is, but for those brought up in a work-ethic culture, it is only puzzling and even somewhat scary.

Bruce Modahl does not only write of the illogic and seeming impossibility of grace. He points also to its ordinariness, its daily-ness, and God's hiddenness in the banal: water, wine, and bread. The sacramental is the visible, the concrete, the ordinary things of this world infused with the spirit to bring us to life.

This sacramental understanding creates the aesthetic of Modahl's theology. He is a pastor, not a poet or a novelist, but his preaching and his writing are rich with story, and his insights come as close to poetry as any pastor's I have ever heard, including the priest-poet John Donne. In this book, Modahl uses stories from his own ministry—stories about both people captured by the Spirit and those in denial. And he uses stories from other writers haunted by grace. These stories are, in Modahl's immersion in narrative theology, actually a means of grace for the reader. They are blessings that empower readers to open their hands to grace freely given. They allow readers to vicariously experience the mistakes and triumphs of others and God's presence in lives anchored to this dear earth even while reaching, stretching to heaven. In short, Modahl's imagination, born in the word of God, enlivens the imaginations of readers. Similarly, he has helped to develop biblical imaginations in those held rapt by his sermons over his many years of ministry. This book, however, is not a collection of sermons. It is, instead, a map for the journey.

Grace may seem risky, uncertain, surprising. But, Modahl assures us, it descends on those who hunger for the crusts and blood of forgiveness. Trust its coming.

Jill Peláez Baumgaertner
Chicago, Illinois
August 2018

Acknowledgments

This book would not have been possible without Jill Baumgaertner, who read every version of every chapter, offering her encouragement, insights, and suggestions. I am grateful to her for her support and friendship.

Phyllis Kersten and Louise Williams critiqued the discussion questions at the end of the book. They offered suggestions so they will better facilitate discussion.

A portion of this book appeared in the December 31, 2015, issue of *The Christian Century*, with the title "Bargaining with Lesser Gods."

Jerry Burce writes the "Thursday Theology" blog for the Crossings Community at www.crossings.org. He kindly invited me to use his blog to hone some of my narratives.

Chapter 1

Prolegomenon

Jack Daniels was a Lutheran. I discovered this when visiting my cousin and his wife in Tennessee. Jack joined Joyful Servants Lutheran Church in Seymour. No doubt for all 84 years of his life people have been saying, "What was his momma thinking when she named him Jack?" She was not thinking Jack; she was thinking John. She was not thinking Tennessee whiskey; she was thinking John, the beloved disciple. In full disclosure, his name is not Jack Daniels, but something like it. The church is not Joyful Servants, but close. And the town may or may not be Seymour. Otherwise the story is as my cousin handed it on to me.

The Lutheran Church in Seymour has had its ups and downs. A group of people organized the congregation almost thirty years ago. They are mostly retirees from up north. They came looking for a place warmer than Michigan but not as hot as Florida. They were looking for someplace lukewarm with a good view, so they settled in Seymour in the foothills of the Great Smoky Mountains. Dollywood is just down the road in Pigeon Forge, and Gatlinburg is nearby if they need some excitement. Mostly, they do not. They grew to about two hundred people and built an attractive little church. After five years, the pastor left for larger challenges, and with him went the first wave of people out. They were dissatisfied

1

with the way worship was being conducted. A new pastor came, and by all accounts was doing a great job. The best way to say what happened to him was he lost his nerve. People were still fighting over which hymnal to use and what hymns to sing and on and on. Everyone said, "This is not the way we did it up north." He did not have any experience. He had no one to talk to who could help him sort out the trivia from the treasure. He lost his nerve. When he went, another wave of people left.

By the time Jack Daniels found them, they were down to twenty people in worship on a good Sunday. They had long since sold their church building. They were on their second storefront location. Soon it would be a third. Owners kept selling buildings out from under them. They relied on retired pastors to take turns preaching. When they weren't available, my cousin filled in, though church headquarters did not like him doing that. When he had the sermon, he had to call it a talk.

What attracted Jack to Joyful Servants is hard to say other than he had been in most other churches in town and wore out his welcome in one after the other. That is a lot of welcome to wear out because there are a lot of churches in this notch on the Bible belt.

Jack presented himself to the people of Joyful Servants as their new evangelist. He would talk to anybody anytime about the Lord. In the grocery store, he asked the lady choosing lettuce next to him if she knew Jesus as her personal Lord and Savior. He stood on the street corner in Gatlinburg and stopped tourists by posing the question, "If you died tonight, would you go to heaven?"

Rather than throw away an old Bible, he took it apart and carried pages with him. At the end of his witness, he handed people a page saying, "Here is a gift for you, a page from the Word of God. I think you will find something helpful in its message."

Someone pointed out to him that random pages from the Bible might not be helpful. And what if you got a good story, Jesus stilling the storm, for example, and the page ended right in the middle of the story, leaving Jesus asleep in the stern of the boat and the disciples crying out in fear?

Jack could see this was a weakness in his method. So he took to handing out pages from old hymnals. He told people, "Here is a blessing for you, a page from a hymnal. If you can't read music, you can read the words. God will bless you."

Some people worried that Jack's brand of evangelism would scare people off. They said, "We need to tell Jack he is not to identify himself as being from Joyful Servants." But someone pointed out, "Folks are not exactly beating the doors down to get in. Let him alone." They did. And so they had their official evangelist, the only Lutheran evangelist working the grocery store aisles and street corners in Seymour and its environs.

Jack lived all his life in the foothills of the Great Smoky Mountains. All his life, Jack attended churches in which people were known to encourage the preacher by calling out, "Amen, brother" or "Praise the Lord." For all the years of his life, that is what Jack did when he heard the word of God preached. The people of Joyful Servants Lutheran Church had never before heard such a thing. That is not the way they did it up north. Hearing Jack call out "Amen" and "Praise the Lord" got on peoples' nerves. People said they didn't hear a word of the sermon because they were on edge, waiting for the next "Amen," and trying to anticipate outbursts of "Praise the Lord" so they wouldn't jump in their seats.

My cousin told me one retired pastor got so flustered by Jack that after the service was over he came over to Jack and shook his finger in Jack's face, saying, "Now listen here. In the Lutheran Church we do not say 'Praise the Lord.'"

That moment may have been the turning point. The story made the rounds. People told and retold it and laughed over it. Jack kept coming to church; the people made room for him.

Jack was also a regular at the Wednesday night Bible study. Joyful Servants was the only church in the area, and probably the entire state, claiming 75 percent of its members in small group Bible study. They regularly had fifteen show up at 7:30 on a Wednesday night. Jack added in his "Amen" and "Praise the Lord" at this gathering as well. On the rare occasions Jack missed Bible study, my cousin placed in the center of the table a battery-powered button he found in a catalogue. Pushing the button triggers a voice calling out, "Praise the Lord."

Jack came to church for three years before anyone saw his wife. He talked about Edna. Folks knew their children had come together to celebrate their sixtieth wedding anniversary. After three years, she showed up at church one Sunday. She told people she came to see the people who put up with her husband. She came back the next Sunday and the Sunday after that and has kept on coming. She told one of the ladies she had not been to church in over thirty years. She said, "You want to know about being shunned, I'll tell you."

To my knowledge, no one asked for the details. There is more to the story than I know. All I know is that here was a wounded soul, starved for the Bread of Life.

Joyful Servants Lutheran Church might not survive. They will never build a megachurch, advertise on billboards leading into town, or broadcast their services on television. However, by the power at work within this stiff-necked people, God accomplished something beyond our imagination.

God so loved the world that he gave the world Joyful Servants Lutheran Church and all other churches before and after. This book is about the church. My point of reference is the Lutheran Church, but the issues this book addresses transcend any one expression of God's church. We know the text "God so loved the world that he gave his only Son" (John 3:16). The church is the body of Christ. So it follows that God gave the church as a sign of God's saving love for the world. Joyful Servants Church often falls short. However, with that same church, God graces us with the new creation.

We distinguish between the sign and the thing signified.[1] The sign is the church as we have it. The thing signified is the fulfillment of God's love in a new creation of love and peace. Such is the promise of God that we believe. At times, through the work of the Holy Spirit, the sign and the thing signified come together to give visible witness to God's promised new creation. I believe this is what we witness with Jack Daniels and Joyful Servants Church. We call this

1. Hinlicky, *Luther vs. Pope Leo*, 106–7.

prolepsis. It is more than a foreshadowing. It is a foresighting, like the transfiguration was for Peter, James, and John. The evangelists, Matthew, Mark, and Luke, record the transfiguration at the halfway point of their gospels and of Jesus' ministry. After the death of John the Baptist, with mounting controversy and opposition, on the road meeting endless crowds of sick and hopeful people, the disciples' vision was downcast, focused on the dirt on their feet. Jesus took these disciples up the mountain and effectively took their chin in his hands, wrenching their vision upward as he gave them a foresighting of his resurrected glory. God likewise graces us with foresightings of God's kingdom come. The culture in which we live is predisposed to deny any such thing. As residents of this culture, we are inclined to go along with its objections.

The three-story universe has collapsed. No longer do we inhabit a world with a supernatural level. Divine beings and forces do not roam an upper floor, coming downstairs from time to time, interrupting life in the ordinary world for good or ill. We know what supposedly happens in the basement, so we filled it up. We now inhabit a ranch home. What goes on in the ranch house is our ordinary lives, with no interference from an upstairs or a basement.

Writing in the last century, Peter Berger notes that twentieth-century culture is increasingly sensate, meaning "empirical," "this-worldly," and "secular."[2] Such increase has not abated in the twenty-first century. Faced with broad academic rejection of the supernatural, biblical scholars attempted to slide from under its label by noting the concreteness and sensate nature of creation, the incarnation, the history of Israel, and the life of Jesus. Under the so-called scientific methodology of higher criticism, these scholars, to one degree or another, attributed the supernatural content of the Scripture to its origin in a more credulous or gullible era.

Our institutions and our culture are increasingly secular. It is widely noted that we live in the post-Christian era. Examples abound. Ernest Gaines's novel, *A Lesson before Dying*, narrates a scene in which the main character walks down the street on a Sunday morning. No one else is out. Everyone is at church, and if not,

2. Berger, *Rumor of Angels*, 1.

they are making themselves scarce, because the cultural mores in that time and place called for church attendance. That is no longer the case. Vestiges of religious observance remain in the religiously named holidays for which schools close and businesses shut down. However, on those days, people go on holiday, not to church. The word *holiday* has lost its reference to "holy day."

Berger refers to the secularization theory of modern culture, "using the word secularization not in the sense of what has happened with social institutions, but as applying to processes inside the human mind, that is, a secularization of *consciousness*."[3] This is evident from research done in congregations in which people do not make reference to what God is doing. Rather people talk about what they are doing. For his PhD thesis, Eric Bodenstab conducted research in four Midwestern congregations of the Evangelical Lutheran Church in America (ELCA). The language used to talk about God was part of his qualitative research. He found that God was "used as the object of a passive verb 64.8% of the time." Pastors and other professional leaders interviewed for the project barely broke 20 percent in the number of times they used God as the subject of an active verb. The members of the congregations studied came in at 10 percent.[4] Bodenstab concludes, "The general trends present across these four congregations still present an image of God that is mostly removed and passive, rather than present and active—a substantial challenge for perceiving the presence of the trustworthy, reliable Jesus and for any sense of god [*sic*] calling us in any way."[5]

The Church Innovations Institute, cited in Bodenstab's work, has conducted as-yet unpublished research in mainline, evangelical, and Pentecostal/Charismatic congregations. In a private conversation with Patrick Keifert, the president of Church Innovations, he said their database for evangelical congregations was smaller, but findings were similar to that of mainline churches.

---

3. Berger, *Rumor of Angels*, 3.

4. Bodenstab, "Actors Are Come Hither," 102.

5. Bodenstab, "Actors Are Come Hither," 105–6.

Pentecostal/Charismatic churches reflected a much greater use of God as the subject of active verbs.

Thomas Altizer famously proclaimed the death of God. That announcement was greeted, according to Berger, with prophetic anger, gleeful triumph, "or simply as an emotionally unprovocative fact."[6] These three, claims Berger, "have in common the recognition that such is our situation—an age in which the divine . . . has receded into the background of human concern and consciousness."[7]

In many ways, we who profess faith in God are operational atheists. We do not see God as evident in our daily lives. For all intents and purposes, God is dead also for us. We generally do not consider our jobs as vocations to which God has called us. We struggle to articulate a connection between Sunday worship and the rest of the week. If we do not talk about what God is doing in our congregations, we cannot be expected to talk about what God is doing in our families and in our lives. When speaking of world events, we do not speak of God being at the helm. And when God is mentioned, we hear cringeworthy comments such as those made by televangelist Pat Robertson who, in late September of 1985, took credit for praying Hurricane Gloria away from Virginia Beach. He also claimed his prayerful prowess over the hurricane as a sign from God that he should run for president of the United States.[8]

The Church Innovations Institute, in its work with congregations, introduces people to the practice of dwelling in the word. Two of the principals of the institute wrote a booklet by that title outlining the practice to discover God as the subject of verbs. The routine questions are: What is God doing in our congregation? What is God doing in our community? What is God calling us to do? Keifert writes, "On the basis of more than 17 years of research on how the Bible actually functions in local churches, we found disturbing realities." Biblical illiteracy was chief among the

6. Berger, *Rumor of Angels*, 1.

7. Berger, *Rumor of Angels*, 1.

8. Bachfeuer, "Pat Robertson"; see also RightWingWatchdotorg, "Pat Robertson."

findings. Moreover, people do not have "biblical imaginations, imaginations that grow out of Scripture."[9] Their finding is that those who dwell in the word "over long periods of time . . . begin to imagine their lives being lived within the life of the living, triune God. Within this imagination, they experience . . . the at-handness of the Reign of God."[10]

Berger finds "signals of transcendence within the empirically given human situation." He discovers these working from experience. He notes that others will begin with the tradition, but says that this route is not fruitful for those who are not already part of the tradition. He suggests five of these signals of transcendence: 1) a propensity for order; 2) play, which suspends the structures of time in ordinary life, aims at joy, and has a sense of eternity; 3) hope for the future, which is common especially at a point of defeat; 4) damnation of what is beyond the pale; and 5) humor, the ability to laugh at the human condition.[11]

Reclaiming a three-story universe, even if possible, would hinder rather than aid in our desire to live faithfully in this age. Let us rather decamp to a more biblical conceptualization for God's presence and power. God exists with us on the same plane in which we live our ordinary lives. God's presence and power are not present in the same manner as are other powers. An analogy may lie in the ten or so dimensions of reality proposed by theoretical physicists. These dimensions are visible in their math, but not to the naked eye. God reveals his presence and power at the cross and in the needs of those who cannot help themselves. God's kingdom exists alongside other ungodly principalities and powers that lay claim to our world and our lives. We have it on good authority these principalities and powers will not last.

Jesus came to inaugurate the kingdom of God. By Jesus' teachings and actions in these latter days, he gives us a foresight of God's kingdom fulfilled. By his death, resurrection, and ascension, the kingdom of God draws near. Jesus said that the kingdom of

9. Keifert, *We Are Here Now*, 68–69.

10. Keifert, *We Are Here Now*, 70.

11. Berger, *Rumor of Angels*, 52–72.

God is at hand. He does not mean in hand. That awaits his coming again. Even then, it will not be in our hands, but we in his. We live in the latter days, the time between Jesus' first advent and his return. At the cross of Christ, the sphere that is the kingdom of God overwhelmed the inimical power of the unholy trinity—sin, death, and devil. Christ's return will mark the consummation of God's kingdom come. The powers hostile to God's rule will be no more. At the cross of our Lord, the devil was mortally wounded. In the meantime, he remains as dangerous as any mortally wounded predator. We now live with one foot in the kingdom of God and the other in that of the hostile powers. We are at the same time sinners and saints. We are saints by virtue of Christ's death and resurrection for us. We are sinners by our inability to break free of our bondage to sin and death. Jesus is the one who sets us free and thereby changes our standing before God, how our lives will turn out, and changes our lives in the present.

The premise of this book is that we live in the overlap of two eras: the one in which sin, death, and devil hold sway and the other being the kingdom of God. The kingdom intersects the old order at the cross, where we find a man, in Paul Scherer's words, "stretched out and taut, until he reaches all the way from 'not my will' to 'but thy will be done.'"[12] With our Lord, we live the tension between the two. We who take up our cross, meaning we who take up our death and follow Jesus, are also the persons stretched out and taut until we reach all the way from "not my will" to "but thy will be done on earth even as it is done in heaven."

The premise of this book is that, as we live in this tension, God provides glimpses of God's kingdom come. God does so

- to encourage our faith;
- to give witness to the continuing encroachment of God's kingdom upon this old order of sin and death;
- to give witness to the victory already won in Jesus' death and resurrection;

12. I made note of this quote while listening to recordings of Paul Scherer's sermons at Princeton Theological Seminary.

- to enlist us as God's agents who seek God's will on earth as it is in heaven;

- to equip us to live in the present according to the ethos of the heavenly city and as its citizens—such equipping includes giving us the senses to detect the kingdom of God present among us and the courage and vocabulary to give voice and pen to what we witness.

Living in the tensions of the last days, God provides glimpses of new life under Jesus' kingly rule.

- God does so through the means of grace: the Lord's Supper of ordinary bread and wine, holy baptism using plain water, and the Word communicated by common words. These most often come together as we come together with others for worship. In worship, God employs music. Gathered together to worship God, God gives us a glimpse of eternity.

- Secondly, God does so through an ethos that makes lively use of the risen Lord in the ministry of reconciliation, which God has entrusted to us.

- A third manner in which God makes himself known is through spiritual experiences.

- As God draws us into active citizenship in his kingdom, the biblical witness to the ethos of the kingdom informs our ethics. Our ethics in turn point toward the kingdom of God.

- We can usually muster the courage to live faithfully through the momentous events in our lives. Courage falters in the details of the day. So it is in the daily, the mundane, pedestrian, prosaic, quotidian, and even banal that God shows us our place in God's momentous story. Banal has an especially ominous sound to it. We hear of the banality of evil. I have never heard of the banality of grace. A banality is something trivial or commonplace. So, God reveals his grace in the banal.

In the chapters that follow, my aim is to make a positive contribution to our seeing and participating in God's kingdom at hand. My aim is to give witness to the banality of grace in our everyday lives: in worship, as we seek reconciliation between individuals and groups of people; in spiritual experiences that are more common to us than we realize; in an ethic informed by the future revealed to us by God; and by lives lived in response to this good future. My method is not only to tell but to show. Years ago, I heard the advice "Don't preach about the gospel. Preach the gospel. Don't preach about the sacraments. Preach baptism; preach the Lord's Supper." Across these chapters, my intent is to show God as present and the difference that makes in our lives.

Chapter 2

The Means of Grace

Pastor Bill Vandemere brought communion to Lyle while he
was in the hospital. The curtains drawn around Lyle's roommate billowed out with the presence of numerous family members
at his bedside. More family members arrived for the roommate.
With their arrival, the curtains swirled like a bagpiper's kilt. The
kisses exchanged and greetings offered in a strange language
sounded as unsettling as the skirl of bagpipes. Overwhelmed,
Lyle's smaller entourage fell silent. Pastor Vandemere proceeded
with the communion service. The words of the liturgy stilled the
chaos on the other side of the curtain. The pastor led them in the
confession and forgiveness and read the Gospel text from that
morning's service. He took the small plate of bread in hand and
recited the familiar words, "On the night in which he was betrayed,
our Lord Jesus took bread, gave thanks, broke it." As he continued, he heard people reciting in unison from the other side of the
curtain. Likewise, when he led the family in the Lord's Prayer, he
heard those on the other side praying. The language was different
(Russian, they later discovered), but the rhythms were the same.
After Pastor Vandemere gave the host to Lyle, a large man on the
other side of the curtain pulled it aside. Bill saw the whole family
lined up and ready to receive the Lord's Supper.

Bill had enough hosts for all. Almost. He had one host left for the man in the bed and his wife. She took it, broke it in half, and communed her husband. Bill's communion kit contained a small chalice and a small bottle of wine. Everyone took a small sip until it came to what Bill surmised was a grandson, middle-school age. He drained what was left. The old man had not yet received. His wife batted the boy on the back of the head, took the chalice, swabbed the cup with her little finger, and communed her husband.

We see in different circumstances what Paul announced for Jew and gentile in Ephesians 2: "Now in Christ Jesus you who once were far off have been brought near by the blood of Christ. For he is our peace; in his flesh he has made both groups into one and has broken down the dividing wall, that is the hostility between us."

I glimpse also the ingathering of the nations of Isaiah's vision.

> On this mountain the Lord of hosts will make for all peoples a feast of rich food, a feast of well-aged wines, of rich food filled with marrow, of well-aged wines strained clear. And he will destroy on this mountain the shroud that is cast over all peoples, the sheet that is spread over all nations; he will swallow up death forever. Then the Lord God will wipe away the tears from all faces, and the disgrace of his people he will take away from all the earth. (Isa 25:6–8)

Holy communion is a foretaste of this meal. At the communion table, the Jordan's flow narrows; the curtain separating what is and what will be is sheer. I can almost hear the voices of my mother and father among the hosts of heaven as they join us in singing the words of Isaiah 6: "Holy, holy, holy Lord, God of power and might." For the communion liturgy in my Lutheran tradition, and in many like mine, we often sing the song of the white-robed martyrs from Revelation 5: "Worthy is Christ, the lamb who was slain."

I brought communion to an elderly lady. She told me, "Sometimes in the afternoon, when I'm sitting alone, I hear a young man singing. He is singing a hymn, but I cannot make out the words. I don't recognize the melody. I have never told anyone about this, not even my daughter. I am afraid she will think I am crazy. I think it is an angel I am hearing. What do you think?"

It is a Post-It-note question. It is as if preachers walk around with these questions adhering to our clothing. They are especially bothersome when witnesses are present. Often we can snatch them from our black shirts and stuff them in a pocket before anyone notices. In this case, there are no witnesses. I answer, "I think that is just what you are hearing." Sometimes, my motive in answering such questions is to offer comfort. In this case, I sought to do that. However, I really do think she was hearing an angel.

I know. I know. "Why would it be a young man's voice? Do angels have gender?"

"Neuroscience demystifies the chronic dwindlings of age."

"She is dreaming angels. Better than dreaming demons."

"There are no such thing as angels."

Let's put all rational objections aside for a moment to consider any body of water with which the reader is familiar. These waters comprise the entire world for their scaly inhabitants. Have we fashioned such a world with our theorems and reasons? I have trouble squaring the limits of such a world with an ever-expanding cosmos. And when seeing the priest elevate the host, I marvel at the only begotten Son who dove headfirst into our pond as just another of us fish.

I have brought to this daughter of God a meal composed of ordinary stuff. And yet it is food for her journey from this realm to the one that will last. This food reenchants our drab landscape, bound as it is by death. The new reality fashioned at the cross and empty tomb has no such boundaries. In reality, she has come close to Jordan's shore, so close that she can hear from the other side of the river. With each passing year, the river narrows. Soon she will be able to make out the words and learn the melodies. The day will come when God's holy angels will swim her into the presence of the choristers—angels and white-robed witnesses gathered around the throne of God and the Lamb. She was issued her white robe at baptism when her swimming began. Now she will join their song.

Perhaps she will sing loud enough for me to hear as I draw closer to the shore.

Jeremy Sisko played the part of Jesus in a CBS television miniseries. A reviewer commented on the way Sisko played the part, "It is as though in the midst of every activity, Jesus is listening for a music that is pitched beyond other ears, and his rhythms are determined more by what snatches of tune he can catch than by the din of noise around him."

Pastor Paul Bretscher wrote an adult catechism curriculum, *The Foolishness of God*, in which he made an analogy between the Hebrew people on their way to the promised land and our lives of faith. The Hebrews made their first water crossing when they passed through the Red Sea, out of slavery and into the wilderness of Sinai. Forty years later, they made their second water crossing through the Jordan River into the land promised to them by God. We passed through the waters of baptism, out of our slavery to sin. The Jordan River has long been a metaphor for the boundary marking our entrance into heaven. We will make our second water crossing into the promised land of heaven at our death or at Christ's return. Our present lives are, then, analogous to the Hebrew people in the wilderness of Sinai. The wilderness is the place the Hebrew people were formed as a people for God. So we are currently being formed as God's people. God provided manna for the Hebrew people to teach them that their God was reliable. The manna was a foretaste of the sufficiency of the promised land, just as the Lord's Supper is for us a foretaste and a foresighting of the heavenly banquet. It is one of the means God uses to form us as a people for God.[1]

I don't think Rick Bragg, being of Pentecostal origins, had the Lord's Supper in mind when he wrote of the prayer said over Thanksgiving meals with his extended family. I do think he had heaven in mind, and all those who have preceded him to the heavenly banquet. He writes,

---

1. Bretscher, *Foolishness of God*.

When I was a little boy, the words seemed to last forever. It seemed like we were walking the Exodus ourselves, one paragraph at a time. Surely, I figured, thousands of little boys had starved to death between the words "Let us pray . . ." and "Amen."

The bad thing was, from where I sat, hands clasped but one eye open, I could see it all; more than that, I could smell it all, this wonderful feast laid out hot and steaming. Today was Thanksgiving, my favorite day on the calendar, better than the Fourth of July, Halloween, and Presidents' Day all lumped into one. The pinto beans bubbled in the battered pot, and hot biscuits rested under a warm towel. There was mashed potatoes, creamed onions, cornbread dressing, macaroni and cheese. And in the middle of it all sat the big turkey, its sides trickling with melted butter, specked with black pepper, so close and yet so far.

I grew up with Pentecostals, and they do not have a short blessing in their lexicon. They are not like some denominations that see prayer as a fixed ritual; the Congregational Holiness go to town with a prayer, and they do not turn loose of one till they have wrung it dry.

My uncle John does the blessing now, and he is a man of honor and brings to us a gentle message of great warmth and dignity. It is a simple prayer of thanks for this one day, for the grace that has allowed us to gather here for one more year. I think anyone, of any faith, or of no faith at all, would see great value in it. It is never too long, this message, though the older and older I get, it is sometimes over much too soon.[2]

The Great Thanksgiving is a recent name given the Eucharistic Prayer, and it is great in length. "Eucharistic" means thanksgiving. It is a Greek word used in the Words of Institution: "Our Lord Jesus took the cup, gave thanks [eukaristesas], and gave it to his disciples." The need to explain what the word "Eucharist" means is the reason many thought it necessary to change the name of the prayer. A prayer enfolding the Words of Institution dates at

---

2. Bragg, *My Southern Journey*, 78–79.

least to the early fourth century.[3] The presiding minister sings the preface, "The Lord be with you." She illustrates by extending her hands. "And also with you," we answer back. A few of us, hesitantly, extend our hands to her. "Lift up your hearts," she continues as she lifts up her hands in encouragement. We assure her, "We lift them to the Lord." And then she sings the Proper Preface, the preface proper to the day or the season. For Christmas, she sings, "It is indeed right, our duty and our joy, that we should at all times and in all places give thanks and praise to you, almighty and merciful God, through our Savior Jesus Christ. In the wonder and mystery of the word made flesh you have opened the eyes of faith to a new and radiant vision of your glory, that, beholding the God made visible, we may be drawn to love the God whom we cannot see. And so, with all the choirs of angels, with the church on earth and the hosts of heaven, we praise your name and join their unending hymn."

We do just that. We are all those who gather on this earth before the God made visible in bread and wine. We join our voices with angel choirs and the white-robed witnesses, who are all the faithful who have preceded us in death. We join with all of them and sing the words of Isaiah 6, the words of the giant six-winged seraphs in the temple, "Holy, holy, holy Lord, Lord God of power and might: Heaven and earth are full of your glory." We bow at the sight of keeping company with Isaiah and the seraphs in the temple. Then the text we sing brings us to the parade route on Palm/Passion Sunday, "Blessed is he who comes in the name of the Lord." We unbend our backs to look up. We make the sign of the cross, for that is where he is headed to secure a blessing for us. We cross ourselves when receiving a blessing.[4] Then comes the heart of the prayer in which we recall God's saving acts for humanity and culminate with what God has done for us in this end of all the ages. We hear the words Jesus spoke at the Supper, words passed on to us. The presiding minister stretches her hands over the bread and wine, praying, "Send now, we pray, your Holy Spirit, that we and all

3. Senn, *Introduction to Christian Liturgy*, 67–71.
4. Senn, *Introduction to Christian Liturgy*, 195.

who share in the bread and cup may be united in the fellowship of the Holy Spirit, may enter the fullness of the kingdom of heaven, and may receive our inheritance with all your saints in light." Then we join together praying the Lord's Prayer and it is time for the altar call. We come forward and thrust our hands out like the beggars we are. The presiding minister presses the bread into my manger-shaped hands, "The body of Christ for you." The assisting minister presents himself in front of me with the cup. I guide his hands to my lips and drink the sweet wine. He says, "The blood of Christ for you." Then it is over. Much too soon.

Through Word and sacrament, God provides for us glimpses of his kingdom come. The Word is first and foremost Jesus Christ (John 1). By extension, the Word is the gospel, the Good News proclaiming Jesus Christ. The Word is also Holy Scripture, called the Enscriptured Word in some traditions. More must be said about how and to what end Scripture is the Word of God. I can demonstrate the need to say more by excerpting a portion of Robert Olen Butler's short story, "Up by Heart."

In Sparta, Tennessee, in the year 1909, Beulah Hudgins read the Bible to her husband Hurshel, who could not read. She read it to him every night until she could report in a postcard to her friend, "Hurshel said he had the Bible up by heart and was fixing to go preaching."[5] For his preaching, Hurshel resolved to give them the Word of God unvarnished. He is not going to leave out the hard parts like other preachers do. For, he says, "This is a fierce neck of the woods, the planet Earth. And God's a roughhouser all right."[6] He sets up a revival tent in a meadow outside of town. He posts flyers. When the day comes, a couple hundred people show up. He plants two friends in the congregation to start off the amens. "And," he says,

> I start to tell them all the holy words that have been running around in me for weeks, about the people of Midian and of Bashan and Hesbon . . . and about all the other cities that were destroyed down to every last woman and

5. Butler, "Up by Heart," 201.
6. Butler, "Up by Heart," 202.

child . . . And I am careful as I preach all this to quote
the words in the books and the chapters and the verses
that's in the holy scripture, and the first few times that
I say something like "we took all the cities at that time
and utterly destroyed the men and the women and the
little ones," Ernest or Roy would give me up an "Amen,"
but that soon stops . . . [A]nd I go on to tell them about
how even if you're worshiping the one true God, you got
to watch yourself. "Cause God said if a guy gathers some
sticks on the Sabbath, kill him. If a guy curses, kill him.
If a child is stubborn kill him. There are no amens about
this . . . [A] few are starting to slip along the rows, kind of
ducking a little, heading for the exit.[7]

On he goes in that same vein as a rush for the exits builds.
Hurshel gave them the unvarnished word without leaving out
the hard parts. I, too, do not advocate leaving out the hard parts.
Rather, the hard and easy parts make sense when we know where
they are pointing. The point of all Scripture is Jesus Christ: him
incarnate, crucified, raised from the dead and ascended into heav-
en for our salvation. The biblical narrative ends with the reign of
God manifest and the one seated on the throne saying, "See, I am
making all things new" (Rev 21:5). One can preach a biblical text,
diligently study and teach a chapter of Scripture, and yet preach,
make conclusions from our study, and teach what is not biblical.
For it to be biblical, any text must be brought before the one who is
its Lord. Through Scripture, God makes Christ known to us, and
God heals troubled consciences.

Read all of Scripture with Jesus Christ looming over the text.
When we do so, we witness and experience God's will done on
earth as in heaven. During each summer's week of Confirmation
Camp, the pastors made time for our own study. One summer, the
week's theme was "The Bible Stories We Did Not Learn in Sunday
School." These included the story about Jephthah and his daughter.
Judges 11 informs us Jephthah was the son of a prostitute. His father, Gilead, had other sons, and when they grew to manhood they
drove Jephthah away, saying, "You shall not inherit anything in

7. Butler, "Up by Heart," 218–19.

our father's house." Jephthah fled. The text says, "Outlaws collected around Jephthah and went raiding with him."

In the ebb and flow of Judges, the people abandon the Lord their God in favor of the gods of their neighbors. The neighbors in turn make war on them. The people of Israel call on the Lord. They put away the foreign gods, swearing to worship the Lord God alone. God raises up a judge who leads them to victory. And so it goes, over and over. This time, however, God does not raise up a charismatic leader as judge to throw off the oppressor. This time the elders of Gilead go searching for a leader and turn to Jephthah. He agrees to lead them only if they accept him as judge over them. God shows approval of these arrangements, for "the spirit of the Lord came upon Jephthah."

The advent of the Spirit of the Lord apparently was not enough for him. "Jephthah made a vow to the Lord and said, 'If you will give the Ammonites into my hand, then whoever comes out of the doors of my house to meet me, when I return victorious from the Ammonites, shall be the Lord's, to be offered up by me as a burnt offering.'"

When he arrived home victorious, the first one out of his house was his daughter, his only child, dancing with tambourine in hand to celebrate his victory. In anguish, Jephthah tore his clothes and said, "Alas, my daughter! You have brought me very low. For I have opened my mouth to the Lord, and I cannot take back my vow." His daughter submitted, asking only for a two-month reprieve so she might wander on the mountains with her friends to lament. At the end of the two months she returned and Jephthah "did with her according to the vow he had made."

The biblical writer spares us the details. Jill Peláez Baumgaertner does not. In the final words of her poem "Jephthah's Daughter," she writes:

> She climbed upon the altar by herself
> and smoothed her gown snagged on the rocks.
> Her friends had garlanded her hair
> so that what met her father's nostrils first
> was not singed hair but chains

of flowers crushed by fire,
this child of God.

The leader of the study broke down as he was reading the poem. We waited for him to regain his voice. He asked us: Why is this text in our Scripture? There is no rescuing angel. Is there any word from God in this text? A word of judgment? A word of promise?

Our discussion skirted the text. We hesitated to follow the trail into its wilderness. We considered the options. Perhaps it's an old folk tale included by the biblical editors as they make their way to the conclusion at the end of Judges and the beginning of 1 Samuel: the word of the Lord was rare in those days, and the people did what was right in their own eyes. Or perhaps the text should be read in the context of Genesis 22, where God rejects child sacrifice.

Someone pointed out that both Abraham and Jephthah were intent on keeping a promise to God. Another commented that Abraham made no promise; he was obeying God's order. And Jephthah received no such word from God.

Perhaps, someone else said, the point is that the Spirit that came upon Jephthah should have been enough assurance for him. A rejoinder came from the other side of the room: the advent of the Spirit wasn't enough for Gideon, or old Zechariah, or Mary for that matter, but they were not judged harshly. Another spoke up, "They asked for signs; they did not make bargains."

The leader asked, "Have any of us ever made a bargain with God that had unintended consequences?" Silence. Then someone spoke up. "I think I have.

"When I took this new call I promised God that I would work as hard as I could. I asked God to bless my efforts. I want to succeed. I want the congregation to grow and flourish. I see my children in the morning, but they are in bed by the time I get home. I am never home for supper. I eat at my desk as I get ready for whatever is happening that night at church. I don't take a day off. I think I am sacrificing my children and my wife." Our time came to an end.

The conversation continued on the back porch later that night. We talked about Luther's warning that no matter what we say, our god is whatever or whoever we fear the most, and whatever or whoever we trust to relieve that fear, and wherever we hang our hearts. We all saw ourselves in the portrait of Jephthah that our friend had held up for us. We fear failure. We trust in our own hard work to counter our fear. We hang our hearts on success.

This was a community of trust in which one man could weep over the poetry he read and another dared to confess his likeness to Jephthah. It was a community in which we spoke God's words of judgment and promise to each other, idolaters all, called back to the baptismal font, where we put our idolatry to death in Jesus' death and seize the promises made to us in that water.

The community that gathered for Bible study began each day by singing Morning Prayer. We encounter Word and sacrament primarily in worship. Communal worship is also a means God uses to give us a glimpse of his kingdom come. We regard the Lord's Supper as a foretaste of the heavenly banquet. Robert Wilken points out the similarities of heavenly worship in Isaiah 6 and Revelation 4. The six-winged seraphs in Isaiah's vision sing "Holy, holy, holy is the Lord of hosts." The four six-winged living creatures of Revelation "Day and night without ceasing sing, 'Holy, holy, holy, the Lord God the Almighty, who was and is and is to come.'" This worship of God continued for the eight hundred years from Isaiah to Revelation. So does the heavenly host worship God to this day and stretching on to eternity.[8] Not only will we join our voices to theirs, we do so every time we gather to worship God with the same words. We don't know the musical setting they use in heaven, but we know the words.

The Bible is the source of most of the words we use in the liturgy. "Worthy is Christ" is also from the heavenly worship reported in Revelation 4–5. "Glory to God in the Highest" is the angel's song to the shepherds. John the Baptizer spoke the words of "the Lamb of God" in order to recommend Jesus to his (John's)

---

8. Wilken, "With Angels and Archangels," 462.

disciples. The trinitarian invocation is a regular feature in the epistles.[9] Wilken says, "Our present worship can be seen as a kind of apprenticeship for what is to come."[10]

In our worship, we seek to reflect the beauty, grandeur, and grace of God. We build the most beautiful worship space we can afford. If we can afford concrete block, that is fine—as long as it is our best. We seek out musical settings for our hymns and liturgies that are most eloquent for our worship of God. We provide accompaniment to nourish the people's song, raised in worship.

In Word and sacraments and their attendants, worship, and music, God gives us glimpses of his kingdom come. God graces us so through the banal, through ordinary words and material elements like bread, wine, water, vocal cords, throat, and tongue, the wood, tin, and brass in organs, violins, oboes, and trumpets. The kingdom of God belongs to such as these.

9. Wilken, "With Angels and Archangels," 463.
10. Wilken, "With Angels and Archangels," 468.

Chapter 3

The Ministry of Reconciliation

Bob Dylan's "The Times They Are A-changin'" was the theme song during the latter half of the 1960s and the early years of the 1970s for those who were later known as the Boomer generation. In their youth, this generation was pro-civil rights, anti-war in Vietnam, and suspicious of authority. The cultural dislocation of parents from their children gave birth to the term "generation gap."

The times were changing in the church. The charismatic movement infiltrated mainline churches for better and for worse. Jesus people were common on college campuses. Clothed in the hippie uniform, they proclaimed, "Get high on Jesus, not on drugs."

A young man in high school found a place in the youth group of the Lutheran Church to which he and his family belonged. This was in one of the larger cities in Florida. Lutheran churches were scarce at that time and in that place; it was an immigrant church. However, Lutherans were not arriving by boat from northern Europe, but by Interstates 75 and 95. The young man and his parents were part of that migration.

At the time, the Lutheran church aimed at its youth an endeavor called Ambassadors for Christ. The youth went two-by-two into the city streets surrounding a particular Lutheran church. They knocked on doors. When those inside answered the knock,

the youth launched into their well-rehearsed pitch. "We are sur-
veying the neighborhood on behalf of (let's say) St. John Lutheran
Church over on Market Street." One of the team carried a pad upon
which he or she made note of the conversation. The first question
was, "Do you have a church home?" If the answer was yes, the duo
said, "If I may ask, what church is that? We are not here to steal
you away from your church. We simply want to know more about
our neighbors."

If the answer was no, the next part of the spiel went along
the lines of, "I want to invite you and your family to visit St. John
for worship at 10:30 on Sunday mornings. Here is a brief flyer that
will tell you more about the congregation. Do you think you might
take us up on our invitation?"

No matter which direction the survey went, the duo drove
the conversation to a final question that came straight from James
Kennedy's *Evangelism Explosion*: "If you died tonight, do you think
you would go heaven?" Whether they answered yes or no, this was
the time when the youth witnessed to their faith: "If I die tonight
I am confident I will go to heaven because I believe Jesus died and
rose again for me and for you for the forgiveness of sins and the
promise of eternal life."

The first church to benefit from their ambassadorship was a
largely African-American Lutheran church in pre-Disney-World
Orlando. The plan was to canvass on Saturday. They went out in
pairs, one black and one white. The white youth spent the night in
homes of members of the congregation. The next day they joined
the congregation for worship. Remember the time and place, the
south in 1967 and 1968, the years of involvement for those youth
and for the young man in the following account.

The ambassadors were dispatched to Jacksonville, Florida in
the summer of 1967 to canvass on behalf of the only other largely
African-American Lutheran congregation in the state. This was to
be a week's worth of canvassing. The black and white youth and
the pastors in charge stayed the week in a motel on a busy road.
Fourteen white and black young men and young women answered
the call. The six boys decided that they wanted to stay together in

one room. When our young man registered at the front desk, the receptionist said, "You know there are negroes in there?" He reassured her, "Yes, I know that. It will be ok."

Later he went to the pool and saw a sign on the gate: "Closed for Repair." He sought out Pastor W. and said, "The pool looks fine to me. The water is clear and the pump is working. What's the deal?"

Pastor W. replied, "That pool is right on the main road. The owner is afraid that if people driving by see black youth in the pool and, worse than that, black youth in the pool with white youth, he would be inviting trouble. The sad thing is he is probably right. The motel owner had to accept us as customers, as much as he would like not to have us. Nothing can stop him from closing his pool."

Pastors W. and S. found a neighborhood pool the ambassadors had all to their own for late-afternoon swimming and fraternizing, as well as vain attempts to dunk Pastor W. He was a big guy.

During this week, a race riot broke out in Tampa. The boys had the television on in the room. But with all the fooling around no one could hear it until someone saw what was happening and shushed the others. They watched in silence and went to bed. The four who drew long straws had the two double beds. They slept head to foot. Smelling one another's feet was preferable to having their heads so close together. It had nothing to do with race but with gender. Queer was an epithet in those days, one every young male dreaded.

At the end of the week, they took the train home. Our young man and his friend and two young women from their congregation served as ambassadors that week. On the way home, they hatched a plan. Soon after returning home, they presented themselves to the pastor, asking his approval to invite youth from an African-American congregation to fellowship together at their congregation. On Saturday afternoon they would play volleyball, have a Bible study, followed by a picnic meal together on church grounds. The pastor said he would take the matter to the board of elders. The board said fine, but these would have to be youth from their particular brand of Lutheran.

The four young people talked it over with one another and their adult advisor. Our young man said, "They all know the closest Lutheran Church with black members is in Orlando. Let's invite them for the whole weekend including church on Sunday and see what happens." And so the plan went forward. They made the invitation to the Orlando congregation. About a dozen youth came from that congregation with adult leaders and joined in volleyball, with a balance of male and female, black and white players on each team. They had a picnic and Bible study. Members of the host congregation housed the visitors for the night and brought them to church the next morning. A half dozen parents came from Orlando for worship, Sunday dinner in the hosts' homes, and to help with the drive home.

After the Sunday dinner and farewells, our young man turned to his father and said, "You see, they have manners and eat with knives and forks just like we do." So began another conflict between our young man and his father. The arguments escalated when our young man's father voted for George Wallace in 1968. There is no justifying our young man's words and actions when he baited his father into an argument. He often was self-righteous, obnoxious, and a know-it-all. He was proud of racial reconciliation, but caused conflict in his own family. He was a hypocrite.

There were other times. His circle of high-school friends often gathered at the Pelican Pool Hall after they got out of school. One of the days they gathered was the day after the assassination of Dr. Martin Luther King Jr. When our young man arrived, McDuff was leading everyone in the hall, cheering King's assassination. He took in what was happening. He stepped around friends until he stood in McDuff's face. He said loudly enough for everyone to hear, "This is not right on any level. You might not like black people or desegregation. But cheering his death is wrong." His friends stopped cheering King's death and started jeering at him. The only thing he could do was walk out the back door and to his car.

City leaders announced the date and time of a commemoration event for Dr. King. It was to be held on the steps of the county courthouse. Our young man decided to go. He did not tell anyone what he was doing. He found parking several blocks away and walked from there. When he got to the courthouse he could not find another white face in the crowd. White people were on the stage. They were the city leaders who had a part in the program. He looked around him and wondered if perhaps he was not welcome. He realized the black woman standing next to him was studying his face as he looked around. She said to him, "It's alright, baby. I am glad you are here."

On the drive home, he realized that the goal Pastors W. and S. had for Ambassadors for Christ was more about bringing black and white youth together and less about the results of our canvassing recorded on those little sheets of paper.

Paul proclaims that, through Christ, "God was pleased to reconcile to himself all things, whether on earth or in heaven, by making peace through the blood of his cross" (Col 1:20). Paul considers the hostility between two groups of people, Jews and gentiles. He reasons that since Jesus reconciled "both groups to God in one body (Jesus' own) through the cross," he therefore broke down "the dividing wall, that is, the hostility between us" (Eph 2:14, 16). Paul moves from the universal to a particular example and on to a charge for Christian ministry. He says, "From now on we regard no one from a human point of view . . . So if anyone is in Christ, there is a new creation . . . All this is from God, who reconciled us to himself through Christ, and has given us the ministry of reconciliation; that is, in Christ God was reconciling the world to himself" (2 Cor 5:16–19). These are grand words spawning grand ideas for racial reconciliation, peace among nations, and harmony in families and in the church. However, the words and ideas come to fruition in the banal, quotidian, and everyday human encounters of those seeking reconciliation.

"I'd rather run naked through the jungle," a pastor said to her coworker, "but we have to do this." They were talking about a peacemaking visit to one of the members of their congregation, Louise, whose father had died. The pastors had had several difficult encounters with Louise in the past, and they knew she was on the outs with her sister-in-law, Patricia. Now they had learned that

Louise had banned Patricia from the funeral. The senior pastor, not as brave as his coworker, did not want this confrontation, but he knew his colleague was right.

When they arrived at Louise's home, her mother was there, along with Louise's sister, Amy, from out of town. The pastors began their visit by rehearsing some of the details of the funeral service. Then the senior pastor said, "Louise, we heard you have banned Patricia from the funeral. We have come to ask you to set aside your differences with her for this one day and let her sit next to your brother for his father's funeral." Her mother, the widow of the man who had died, turned to her daughter and also asked her to let her sister-in-law sit with the family for the funeral. Amy made the same plea. Louise's face and eyes reddened. She cried in anger as she rehearsed all her sister-in-law's faults. "No," she said, "and if she comes to our pew, my sons will escort her out."

By the time the pastors made the five-minute return trip from their house to the church, a message from Louise's husband, Manny, screaming at the pastor, had been left on the pastor's phone. Later that day, he told Patricia he could not force her on her husband's family, but they could not ban her from the funeral. She said she did not want to make a scene, but would feel even worse if she sat apart from the family. On the day of the funeral, she came after the family took their seats. She stood in the narthex and watched. The Lord's Supper was not part of this liturgy. The only peace evident in that liturgy came at the commendation.

Two weeks after the funeral, the pastors met at the church with Louise and Manny, who brought their former pastor with them. Their anger had only grown. They claimed the pastors needed to apologize for causing Louise distress. Manny became so angry that he stood up and reached across the table towards the senior pastor to shout as close to his face as he could get. They left the church to return to another congregation. Months later the senior pastor received a lonely email from Louise with no greeting and no name at the end. It said: *Would you not leave the ninety-nine for the one sheep?* In his reply he asked her to read the whole passage, Luke 14:34—15:7. The final verse reads, "There will be more joy in heaven over one sinner who repents than over ninety-nine righteous persons who have no need of repentance." He wrote, "Pastor A. and I did what the shepherd did. We came out to you and asked you to change your mind. We asked in a kind way. Are you ready now to make amends with Patricia?" He never heard from her again. Years later he heard that Louise had apologized to her sister-in-law. Louise and Patricia reconciled, which led to reconciliation within the extended family. The pastors will never know if their visit that day had a part to play in their peace-making.

The pastor is sometimes not the one seeking reconciliation, but the one in need of it. A certain pastor met with a committee searching for a youth minister. Several committee members were forceful and held strong opinions about youth ministry, not all of which were well-founded. They and the pastor clashed from the beginning. As the search dragged from one year to the next, relations deteriorated between the pastor and the leaders of the committee. The chair of the committee said the pastor's contribution to committee meetings consisted mainly of eye-rolling and sighing. The pastor defended herself, claiming that the committee was interviewing inappropriate people, and did not ask for her input nor recognize her expertise. Finally, the pastor said, "I'm done." Her colleague said, "I understand that. I will meet with the committee from now on. But it is important for you to meet with them one more time. You can tell them your frustrations. They may not even know why you are upset with them and why you are no longer part of the committee. They also can tell you their concerns. It would be a good thing to seek reconciliation with them. We are, after all, called to a ministry of reconciliation." The pastor reiterated her first statement: "I'm done."

Reconciliation is hard work. It often feels like death. Fully vested for Passion/Palm Sunday, a pastor sat in the transept waiting for the prelude to end. Out of the corner of his eye, he saw several women coming up the side aisle in his direction. From the look on the face of the woman in the lead, he knew that she was not happy. She bent down inches from his face and shouted, "Did you tell the minister of music . . . ?" He said he did not remember anything else she said. The only thing he could say was the word "No." He sat among members of the congregation. He was humiliated and ashamed. He does remember thinking, "I wish I was dead." Later he wondered if perhaps she was just trying to speak above the music. She came to see him later in the week. She said he had given an improper instruction to the minister of music and that in his answer to her from under the transcept he tried to shift the blame. She said he lied. He accepted the accusation. He apologized. Then he told her, "No one has screamed in my face like that since kindergarten. I was humiliated right there in the midst of the congregation." She apologized to him. He accepted. They shook hands. He thought all was well, but that was not the case. She looked the other way when they met on the sidewalk or in the grocery store. He sent a letter to her, inviting her continued participation in presenting the children's sermons. She sent the letter back with "I am no longer available" scrawled on the bottom. He called and left a message on her answering machine. She did not return his call. Months went by. Too many months. Finally, he contacted her husband and asked to meet with both of them. He went to their home in the evening. However, the meeting did not go well, and there was no resolution between the pastor and the woman. There is often no resolution in efforts to reconcile with another person. The pastor told me that it was another of those times in his life in which he thought, "I wish I was dead."

We say such things not meaning them literally. There is more truth to them than we want to admit, however. Speaking for myself, I want to be right. When cornered, like the Artful Dodger in *Oliver Twist*, I try to get away. I dodge by shifting the blame elsewhere. It is an old story. "Adam, have you eaten from the tree of which I commanded you not to eat?" And Adam said, "The woman gave it to me to eat." Eve said, "The serpent told me to eat of the tree. In fact, God, the serpent which tricked me is the one you created to be crafty." Follow the logic, and their alienation from God ends up being God's fault. But it is their disobedience towards God that led them to a crack in their relationship with each other. And it is the same for us. Our estrangement from God is the basis for every offense given or received from another. I resist any accusation because I hear in it the echo of God's accusation. I do not measure up. I must dodge God's accusation because that one brings with it a death sentence.

Confession of sins is a regular part of worship. In the order for confession with which I am most familiar, we say, "We are captive to sin and cannot free ourselves. We have sinned against you [God] by thought, word, and deed, by what we have done and by what we have left undone. We have not loved you with our whole heart; we have not loved our neighbors as ourselves." The consequence of our estrangement from God is eternal. The only reason we are able to confess our sins to God is because we know God, "in his mercy has given his only Son to die for us, and for his sake forgives us all our sins." If estrangement between us and God is at the base of all estrangement, when Jesus makes peace between us and God, then the basis for our estrangement with one another is no more. However, while there may be no basis for it, the estrangement does not simply go away. We should not expect reconciliation to be easy when our reconciliation with God came at such great expense.

I noticed a stranger in the back pew one Sunday. I keep my eye out for strangers. He was gone by the time I got out to shake hands at the end of the service. But he was back the next Sunday, and the next. He made himself known by coming up for communion. But he always slipped out at the last hymn. He never wrote his name in the fellowship pad. He was like the homeless at the homeless shelter who come to sleep within the safety of the walls of the patio built just for them. They come inside for a shower and to wash their clothes and for a meal. But they will not register their names or stay inside overnight. They are wary. They aren't sure what might happen to them. They don't trust anyone enough. This man was like that.

One Sunday, though, he stayed through the final hymn and came through the line to introduce himself. He was Don—just Don. That was the Sunday he heard me say in my sermon on Luke 3:7–18 that we need to die. I didn't tell them they needed to change.

I told them, "The old sinner we are, the old Adam and Eve, need to die." But the Holy Spirit filtered out the qualifiers. All Don heard was "You have to die." And he knew it was the truth.

Some months before, Don had walked out on his wife of more than twenty years. He stretched thin the bonds of their marriage with a string of affairs. He had two daughters: one in high school, the second just finishing college. He walked out on them, too. He described nights of debauchery (his term) at one of those places advertised in half-inch ads at the bottom of the sports pages.

His older daughter was planning her wedding, and she called him. She wanted him to walk her down the aisle. She didn't ask for money. She only wanted him to be part of the wedding. She wanted him in her life. That brought him back in proximity with the church. Not a physical proximity to the church to which he belonged. He couldn't walk back into that place. But picturing the wedding in the church where he and his family had worshiped all those years got him thinking about the songs and words and the kind of man he had hoped to be. His daughter's call and her wedding brought him back in conversation with his wife. In one of those conversations, she said to him, "Come home, Don. Just come home."

The effect this had on him—his daughter's kindness and his wife's invitation—forced him to look at the kind of man he had become. He was disgusted with what he saw. That disgust was the means the Holy Spirit used to get him to cross town to hear this comfortably middle-class pastor (who didn't even know he was impersonating John the Baptist that day). Don was already in the wilderness. When he heard me say "You need to die," he knew it was the truth. And so, he died with Christ.

That offer was in my next breath. After saying "You need to die," I said, "Come die with Christ and rise with him forgiven and changed." Hearing this is why he stayed to introduce himself to me. And it's why he came to see me the next day the way those who heard John came to see him. The word of judgment is good news when it is coupled with forgiveness and repentance.

The next day, toward the end of a long conversation with me, Don asked, "What shall I do now?" I led Don into the nave and stood with him by the baptismal font. I handed Don a copy of the worship book as I grabbed one for myself. I asked him to turn to the brief section called "Individual Confession and Forgiveness." I asked, "Are you prepared to make your confession?" Don said he was. Together we read verses from Psalm 51, concluding with "Have mercy on me, O God, according to your loving kindness; in your great compassion blot out my offenses. Wash me through and through from my wickedness, and cleanse me from my sin."

At my invitation, Don summarized what he had told me in my study. Together we read more of Psalm 51: "Create in me a clean heart, O God, and renew a right spirit within me. Cast me not away from your presence, and take not your Holy Spirit from me. Restore to me the joy of your salvation and uphold me with your free Spirit." I asked him, "Do you believe that the word of forgiveness I speak to you comes from God himself?" He answered, "Yes, I believe." Following the order of service, I laid hands on him and said, "God is merciful and blesses you. By command of our Lord Jesus Christ, I, a called and ordained servant of the Word, forgive you your sins in the name of the Father, and of the Son, and of the Holy Spirit." As I said the words "the Son," I marked his forehead with the cross. I reminded him that this cross was first traced on us at our baptisms. It is traced on us in ashes every Ash Wednesday. I said "Peace be with you."

"And also with you," he replied as we shook hands. We stood looking at each other. Don asked, "What shall I do now?" I said, "This is not hard. The answer to this is obvious. Go home. Your wife has called you home. Take it as God's voice gathering you home. Your shame has turned to rejoicing." He did. He went home. He walked his daughter down the aisle. The father of the bride often sheds a few tears as he walks his daughter down the aisle. Usually, however, he does not bawl his head off, as Don did from the moment his daughter slipped her arm into his.

I had a different encounter with a young man raised in the congregation who sought me out after a brief stint in jail. His wife was ready to leave him and take their little boy with her. He told me he'd made a bargain with the devil. He had pledged his life in return for the drugs he craved and sold. I took him to the baptismal font, and we read through the service of Holy Baptism, the covenant God made with him that predated the one he made with the devil. When I asked him, "Do you renounce all the forces of evil, the devil, and all his empty promises?" he responded with a firm, "I do." We then huddled together over the words of individual confession and forgiveness.

I asked him to come back the following week, but I did not see him again. The drugs were his first love. They seduced him and lured him to the grave, as do all lesser gods. Does the baptismal tide have the power to wash him safely to heaven's shore? I assured his parents and myself that it does. He hung his heart on those drugs. God in Christ hung his heart on him.

In the kingdom of God there is no more judgment, since all is finally and completely reconciled in Christ. God effects God's will on earth when husband and wife are reconciled. God's grace is also evident in our unsuccessful attempts at achieving reconciliation. Even the refusal to seek reconciliation points us to what will be. The ministry of reconciliation extends to relationships within the church. Paul wrote his letters to reconcile differing factions within the churches and groups at odds with him.

One pastor repeatedly and in settings as varied as sermons, Bible study, and church council meetings reminded his parishioners that their unity was founded on their faith in Jesus Christ. That gave them the ability to discuss social issues because their unity did not depend on agreement on these issues, but rather rested on Jesus Christ. He said that Jesus is the foundation on which the Spirit of God builds their faith and their congregation. He repeatedly used James Gustafson's memorable phrase, saying they were a "community of moral discourse." His talk was put to the test when a number of members caucused and brought to the board of elders a concern over the congregation's sponsorship of a Boy Scout troop because of the Boy Scout's prohibition of homosexual members and leaders. The church had sponsored the troop for over sixty years. Fathers, sons, and grandsons of the congregation had passed through the troop. As the board took up the issue, the pastor presented them with what he called "ecclesial principles" to guide their discussion. These included the following:

- We recognize our unity is in Christ Jesus and not in clan, race, political views, or opinions on social issues.

- With our unity in Christ Jesus, we have a firm foundation upon which to build a community of moral discourse.

- In such a community, we engage in a free and open discussion about the issues facing our community and world. We will never engage in *ad hominem* arguments or question the Christian faith of another because they hold a different opinion. We can live with the tension of holding and voicing different opinions on political and social issues and how we interpret particular passages of Scripture because we are united on the solid foundation of Jesus Christ.

- We will operate according to Jesus' instruction in Matthew 13. Our task is to throw out the gospel net and pull in all who come. We are not to make decisions on the worthiness of some over others. We will adhere to the call of God's prophet: "Ho, everyone who thirsts, come to the water" (Isa 55:1).

- All are welcome. Such is integral to the character of the gospel.

Over a period of six months, the board approached the issue by inviting servants of the church who were biblical scholars, theologians, and social scientists representing both sides of the issue. The congregation was kept informed of the discussion. The consensus of the elders was that the congregation should have the same opportunity to hear from and interact with these seminary professors and Bible college teachers. Before doing so, the pastor held a three-Sunday adult forum with the awkward title of "How We Discuss Divisive Social Issues." He used his "ecclesial principles" as the basis for the three sessions. Approximately sixty people filled the seminar room to its capacity for three August Sundays.

At the end of the third Sunday, the pastor asked people to name all the controversies facing church and society. When the whiteboard was full, the pastor told everyone to take three stickers and affix them to three of the issues they thought needed to be addressed by the congregation. The three listed in the order of votes received were 1) the recently initiated first war in Iraq; 2) the authority of Scripture; 3) and homosexuality.

A small task force set to work on designing the conversation around each issue. For the war in Iraq, a panel was recruited consisting of three people: a Jesuit theologian to present on the just war doctrine, a leader of the Lombard Mennonite Peace Fellowship, and a professor from an evangelical college. This forum took place on a Sunday morning. For the conversation on the authority of Scripture, a theologian from a nearby Lutheran university led the discussion on four successive Sunday evenings in August. The pastor set up for twenty people. Seventy-five people showed up, with an average attendance of fifty-five for the four evenings.

The task force designed a more elaborate format for the discussion on homosexuality. Representing opposing views, biblical scholars, theologians, and social scientists came one at a time for events that began with lunch following the 11:00 a.m. Sunday worship service. The fifth and final event was held on a Sunday evening. Gay and lesbian members of a Lutheran congregation were invited to speak about their faith and their families, their experiences with the church, and the hospitality of the congregation to which they belonged. It was at this event where one member of the congregation told the pastor that it seemed the discussion was being driven to a foreordained conclusion. The pastor said that was not his intent, nor was it the intent of the task force. However, since the topic involved people, it was necessary to form opinions in the face of those affected. At the end of these discussions, no votes were taken. What did emerge was the affirmation that everyone was welcome.

One conversation the pastor related is telling. A member met with him in his office. He told him that his mother-in-law left her congregation over this issue, and he and his wife would do the same if this congregation went down the same path. The pastor asked him if he thought gay and lesbian people should be welcomed to worship. The man said, "Of course." The pastor asked him if he thought they could become members. After a brief hesitation the man said, "Of course." The pastor said, as he had publicly and in varied places, that the congregation did not have a doctrinal quiz for people to take upon entering worship or coming to the Lord's Supper. The congregation would likewise not quiz people on their sexual preferences as they came in the door. While some congregations display a rainbow as the sign that they are inclusive, the cross is the ultimate sign of the reconciliation we proclaim. Everyone is welcome here.

The ministry of reconciliation is also at the heart of the church's public ministry to the world. A congregation invited consultants from the Church Innovations Institute to facilitate the Institute's process of "congregational discovery." In the course of this guided self-study, the congregation asked what the pastor called "the three essential questions": What is God doing in the community around us? What is God doing in our congregation? What is God calling us to do? Several people heard God calling the congregation to host forums for the community to discuss social issues. The pastor saw the congregation making the step from being a community of moral discourse to becoming also a public moral companion for the community. To those who came to him with the idea, he gave permission to proceed, as well as copies of *Testing the Spirits: How Theology Informs the Study of Congregations*, asking them to read Gary Simpson's essay "God, Civil Society, and Congregations as Public Moral Companions."

Simpson notes the rage dominating our civil landscape, putting great stress on civil discourse and institutions. He hears the church being called to serve in a public vocation to provide the space and the setting for a civil conversation in matters affecting all citizens of the community, so long as the conversation is conducted in a considerate and kind way. The church seeks to address the moral issues in the various items roiling our democracy.[1] Simpson

1. Simpson, "God, Civil Society, and Congregations," 67–72.

summarizes with certain marks "that characterize the congregational vocation of serving as a public moral companion." These are "a *conviction* that they participate in God's ongoing creative work . . . A *compassionate commitment* to other institutions and their moral predicaments . . . [and] a *critical* and *self-critical*—and thus a fully *communicative*—procedure for moral engagement."[2]

Those who first approached the senior pastor with the idea chose the name "Faith Perspectives" for themselves and the forums they developed. They invited others to serve. In the course of five years, dozens of people cycled in and out of the central committee, and dozens more served as table discussion leaders and resource people. The topics addressed in Faith Perspective forums were: the Great Recession, immigration, health care policy, Palestine and Israel, and violence against women. The first and last forums were single events, while the others took place in both fall and winter. The committee recruited presenters to give background information and to represent different points of view. They discovered that it was often difficult to find people willing to share a microphone with certain other people. However, they persevered, and brought together seventy to one hundred people from the congregation and community for Saturday morning forums. The table discussion resulted in questions for the presenters that were both pointed and polite.

These engagements in the ministry of reconciliation clearly reveal that the kingdom of God is not fully upon us. They do show us, however, a glimpse of God's kingdom, where the reconciliation God effected at the cross of Jesus is fully realized. They also demonstrate the power of God's reconciling love at work in the everyday lives of people, congregations, and communities.

---

2. Simpson, "God, Civil Society, and Congregations," 88.

Chapter 4

Spiritual Experiences

Thick glass magnified his eyes. His eyeballs danced from one side to the other, up and down, and spun around. He looked like a road sign, his body the size of the pole holding up a stop-sign-sized head, altogether around six feet tall. He snatched up any piece of paper that came close to his desk, unfolding and holding it an inch or so from his eyeglasses. He reminded me of a character on TV or in the movies who sticks an eyepiece in one eye to assess precious stones. But there was nothing precious in what Larry examined. At first, they were bits of stray paper. But once his classmates, not all of us by any means but enough of us, witnessed his compulsion, we took advantage of any reason to walk by his desk and drop tightly folded notes on it. He held them to his eyes and carefully unfolded them and smoothed out the paper on the desk so he could read insults from his fellow ninth graders.

"You are weird."

"Does your mother buy your clothes from Goodwill or the Salvation Army?"

"You look like a turd."

"The best entertainment of the day is watching you unfold and read the latest gem from your classmates."

"Why bother unwrapping these notes? Why don't you just throw them away?"

I figured the last one was from a girl in the class, the only girl I ever saw drop a note near him. I read them all—at least, all of those that came to him during homeroom, where I sat directly behind him.

I had a couple other classes with Larry. In science class, the lab tables were square blocks with sinks at one corner and Bunsen burners at each work area. Each table had room for five or six of us. I drew Larry as my lab partner. At our table, learning to work as a team came in as a distant second to tormenting Larry. We took every advantage we could to carry out this work.

The Ghost of Christmas Past brings me to one day in particular. The teacher said, "I have to talk to Mr. Kirby for a minute. I trust you to stay on task when I am not in the room." We stayed on task all right.

"Larry. Nobody names their kid 'Larry.'"

"The only other Larry I know is one of the Three Stooges."

"Are you one of the Three Stooges?"

"You got brothers named Moe and Curly?"

"Maybe your middle name is Moe: Larry Moe Taylor."

"My middle name is John."

"What is wrong with your eyes?"

"I have a congenital condition."

"What is that?"

"It means I was born with it and it is hereditary. This particular condition affects males and it skips generations. My grandfather had it, but my father has normal vision. If I should ever have a son, he would have normal vision, but his son would have what I have."

"How stupid are your parents? They could have helped clean up the gene pool by not having any kids. By not having you," I said. And when I said it, I saw Larry tear up. This was the first time I ever saw him do that. It made his humiliation all the worse. It egged us on to more of the same. And I did it to him. This was my first sin of commission in the torment of Larry John Taylor. Prior to that, they were all sins of omission because I stayed silent and did not interrupt the torment.

Larry and I should have been allies. We both lived on the lonely margin of life in the ninth grade. I was the chubby kid, also six feet tall. One kindly classmate said, "Oh, you still have some baby fat." No doubt true. Very little of that weight was muscle. A girl beat me at arm wrestling. That may not be so rare then or now, but in the mid-1960s, that was humiliating. And I was a newbie. We moved into this Florida city during the summer. Prior to this I went to school with the same Midwestern neighborhood kids from kindergarten through the eighth grade. We all grew up in the shadow of the International Harvester plant in post-World War II box houses. We wore what our parents bought us and took little notice. The kids in this new school enforced a rigid dress code. I did not get the memo that boys must wear Gant shirts, Bass Weejun penny loafers, Gold Toe socks, and London Fog jackets for cold days.

Larry got a cupcake with a candle pressed into the center of it as classmates sang happy birthday to his pants. This was after he wore them for ten days straight. I was glad they did not have their eyes on me because I wore the same pair every day for many more than ten days. What perhaps saved me was that I did have two Gant shirts I received as going-away presents at a surprise party my friends had for me shortly before we moved. And at Christmas I got two new pairs of pants from a store that was not Montgomery Ward or Sears. So, Larry and I had much in common. We knew that if we margin-dwellers got pulled into the center of attention, it meant misery. Larry was an easy target. I would do anything, even join in his torment, to avoid that.

I have acknowledged I did nothing to counter the abuse Larry received. But there was another boy who did. Keith sat at a lab table next to ours. He overheard the delight we were taking in filleting Larry. Keith got up from his chair and slid into a vacant seat at our table. I thought I recognized him from somewhere other than this science class, but I could not put my finger on it.

He paused to look each one of us in the eyes before saying, "Stop it. Stop picking on Larry. He did nothing to make his eyes the way they are, and he has done nothing to deserve your abuse." He slid from our table and back to his own just as the teacher walked back into the room.

The following Sunday I was in my place in the tenor section of the choir. The choir director made a place for three of us teenagers in the senior choir. And it was one of a few places I found refuge that year. From this perch in the choir, looking all holy in my white robe, I saw Keith coming into church with his family: mom, dad, and two sisters. They came in the side door. As they turned into the main aisle of the nave, Keith looked back to me. As I looked down, the shame rose over me.

Many of us remember that the loneliest and most vulnerable time of day was lunch. In the spring of the year, it came to the attention of the powers-that-be that Larry was at the back corner table as usual, but now with female company. Pearl Spillman sat across from him. I probably don't have to tell you this, but Pearl was the only one with that name in the school, and probably in the whole state if you did not include grandmas in the counting. She dressed like someone's grandma, long skirts and blouses with ruffles going down the front. Furthermore, Pearl's father dropped her off in front of school every morning driving his work truck with Spillman Upholstery painted large on the sides and back. We all knew the code for getting to and from school. You do not ride a bicycle. If one of your parents brings you, they drive something that does not draw attention unless the vehicle is a Corvette or some such car. Somewhere in the middle of the code were those who had a "motor." A "motor" was what we called a scooter with a fifty- (or better yet, a ninety-) cubic-inch motor. Most of us walked.

For a while, it looked like Larry and Pearl's courtship was going to pass unremarked. That was not to be. After lunch, most of us went outside to the picnic tables next to the basketball court to wait for the bell to ring. No one ever had a picnic at these tables. They were made of concrete embossed with the name of the mayor of the city. That was not so unusual. His name was pressed into every sidewalk, bridge, or street that was built or fixed during his time in office. After he died, they named a street after him in the worst part of town. This being Florida and already hot, everyone tried to find a seat on one of the stone picnic tables in the shade. We sat on the table tops with our feet on the bench where normal people sit. That's just the way it was done. One day Pearl was sitting on one of the picnic tabletops and Larry stood in front of her. He stood close so he could see her as they talked. Brad presented himself in front of them. Brad was one of the more popular kids. He played football. Sometimes coaches prepare their team for an opponent by telling them, "They are big, but they are slow." Brad was big and fast and strong. He took most of the handoffs from the quarterback. His girlfriend was the head cheerleader. They were blond and beautiful people. Junior high school, the birthplace of clichés.

On this day, Brad started in on Larry and Pearl. "Larry and Pearl, you are such a lovely couple." Brad talked loud. He was putting on a performance he wanted all of us to see and hear. "Pearl, you are so be-yooo-ti-ful. You are the prettiest girl in the whole school." Brad got down on his knees. "Pearl, if Larry could spare you for just one date I would love to take you out. Larry, you are such a lucky guy. If only you could see her gorgeous big nose and her grandma clothes." He went on and on in that loud voice. No one interrupted Brad. Everyone out there was still and silent and embarrassed. I sat there hoping that the bell would ring, calling us to class, and put an end to it.

Keith came around the corner of the cafeteria. He stopped and looked until he could figure out what was going on. He walked over and stood between Brad and Pearl. "Stop it," he said to Brad.

"What are you going to do about it?" answered Brad.

"Just what I am doing. I'm stopping you from acting like a fool and humiliating these people."

Brad squared up in front of Keith and balled up his fists. Keith said, "I know you are stronger than I am and a half-head taller. No doubt you can beat me in a fight if that is what you want. If that is what you want, I'll give you one."

For a few hour-long seconds, they stared at each other. Brad said, "I was only having some fun. I didn't mean anything by it." And he walked away.

The bell rang, calling us to class.

The next day at lunch time, Larry and Pearl were alone at their same table in the corner of the cafeteria. I was close by at another of those tables with a nerdy friend, eating fast, hoping no one would take notice. Keith came out of the lunch line with his tray. He walked past all his friends and went to the corner table. "Mind if I sit here?" he asked Pearl and Larry.

"No, of course not," answered Pearl.

Keith took a seat at the other end of the table. He ate by himself. Pearl and Larry talked in quiet tones only they could hear.

Keith kept at this for several days in a row. His friends called to him as he carried his lunch tray by them. "Come on, Keith. Sit with us." Keith kept walking to the corner of the lunchroom to his seat at the end of the table with Larry and Pearl at the other end.

Keith continued to ignore his friends' call to join them for lunch. They asked him, "Why are you doing this? Look around, buddy. You know you are committing social suicide."

He broke his silence to answer, "I don't want to sit with a bunch of cowards."

It went on like this for a couple more weeks. Finally, Laura, who was Keith's girlfriend, came to the corner table and asked if she could join them. Pearl said, "Of course."

Keith introduced Laura to them. Keith asked, "Would it be ok if we move closer to you so we can talk together?"

Pearl answered, "We would like that."

It did not take long before another friend of Laura and Keith asked to sit with them. And then another and another. The table filled. Soon they needed more space. They asked us if they could sit at our table. "By all means," I said. Some awkward apologies to Larry and Pearl followed.

It was not social suicide. It felt more like some sort of new creation—at least of one corner of junior high. The apostle Peter said, "You are a chosen race, a royal priesthood, a holy nation, God's own people" (1 Pet 2:9). Whenever I think of Keith, I remember this verse, and vice versa. He made it possible for many of us, if just for a short period of time, to live up to what Peter says we are: a royal priesthood, a holy nation, God's own people.

This story unfolded over the better part of a school year. For me, it was a profound spiritual experience in which God spoke words of judgment and grace to me that have stayed with me ever since.

Diogenes Allen asked his class at Princeton Seminary if any among them had had a spiritual experience. No one raised a hand. "Just as I thought," said Dr. Allen. He added that he was actually quite certain most of us had had such transcendent experiences. As evidence, he cited a class exercise undertaken by Michael Pafford who taught a poetry class to five hundred upper form (freshmen) students in England. Pafford was preparing to teach the poetry of Wordsworth, but wondered if it would mean anything to his students. In order to find out, he printed out and gave to his students an example from a novel of an unusual experience, such as one encounters in Wordsworth's poetry.

Allen writes about this tale in what he calls his "spiritual autobiography," although he does not mention which poems Pafford cites. However, we know that Wordsworth encounters the divine in nature. In his poem "Tintern Abbey," he writes of the forests and fields that comprise for him an abbey, a place where one discovers the sacred. There,

> with an eye made quiet by the power
> Of harmony, and the deep power of joy,
> We see in the life of things.

His encounter with nature confirms

> Our cheerful faith, that all which we behold
> Is full of blessings.

As with Wordsworth's poetry, Allen does not reveal what example Pafford supplied his students from a contemporary novel. An appropriate choice would be a scene from *Mr. Ives' Christmas* by Oscar Hijuelos. Ives received assurance that all was right with the world, not from viewing forests and fields, but from the most ordinary of circumstances. After climbing out of a stalled elevator, "the nine or so people gathered on that floor seemed to be radiating what Ives could only define as goodness, as if they were angels, sent to reassure him during a crucial moment of doubt."[1] Out on the corner of Madison and Forty-First streets, "Ives was waiting for the light to change, when he blinked his eyes and, in a moment of pure clarity that he would always remember, began to feel euphoric."[2] He believed that he had been "privy to the inner workings of God."[3]

Pafford asked his students if they had had such an experience and to describe it if they had. Allen writes,

> To his amazement, over fifty-five percent answered, 'Yes,' and proceeded to tell him about it . . . [V]irtually none of them had told anyone about it before, and all of them felt that the moment or moments were extremely important. Half of them had no idea what to make of their experiences. The rest understood them as experiences of the presence of God . . . God was reaching out and touching young lives, utterly uninvited.[4]

Allen spoke to us of his own experience hearing a word from God. It happened in the course of *lectio divina*. The Latin phrase for this ancient spiritual practice means "reading divine things." He read Psalm 139 and was struck by verses 20–22: "They talk blasphemously about you, regard your thoughts as nothing. Yahweh, do I not hate those who hate you, and loathe those who defy you? I hate them with a total hatred, I regard them as my own enemies" (NIV). Following the rubrics for *lectio divina*, he repeated these verses over and over to himself. He thought of the place he teaches, what his colleagues say about God, and what is said at the conferences he attends. He writes,

> All too often, it seemed to me, my fellow theologians "blasphemed" and "regarded as nothing" God's thoughts

1. Hijuelos, *Mr. Ives' Christmas*, 99.

2. Hijuelos, *Mr. Ives' Christmas*, 100–101.

3. Hijuelos, *Mr. Ives' Christmas*, 106.

4. Allen, *Steps Along the Way*, 5.

as revealed in scripture. I realized I did hate them, and believed my anger and hatred well-founded. Suddenly it occurred to me that perhaps God did not regard them as his enemies, even though I did. My mind and heart began to be stretched by this possibility. If God did not regard them as his enemies, then they could not be my enemies either.[5]

The next rubric in *lectio divina* calls for prayer. In his prayer, Allen asked for forgiveness and God's assistance in his dealing with colleagues and students. A few hours later, Allen experienced peace and joy. Better yet, his relations with colleagues changed. He continued to criticize ideas with which he disagreed, but he did so without anger. He discovered he was now taken more seriously than before.[6]

Allen cautioned his class that if any spiritual experience they have is from God, it will conform to Scripture, understood as fulfilled by Jesus Christ. He wrote, "The Word of God spoken at creation is the source and organizing principle of the cosmos. The same Word that was spoken by God at creation shines in our hearts so that we may have knowledge of God by looking to Jesus Christ. Scripture is the witness or testimony to that Word in creation, in our hearts, and in Jesus Christ."[7]

Allen raises the question of why we hesitate to acknowledge that we have spiritual experiences. Moreover, even when we do, we resist giving the details. In one pastor's Transfiguration Day sermon, she told her congregation that she had a mountaintop experience one summer at camp, but she did not tell us what the experience was. She said, however, that she did tell her camp counselor. Her camp counselor told her never to tell anyone else. What makes us so reluctant, so hesitant, to address this issue? I, for one, hesitate to talk about spiritual experiences because I have seen how others use their own closeness to God to manipulate people. How can you argue with someone who has heard directly from God? My regular

5. Allen, *Spiritual Theology*, 87.

6. Allen, *Spiritual Theology*, 87–88.

7. Allen, *Spiritual Theology*, 138.

advice is to be suspicious of anyone who claims to know exactly what someone else should be doing because they heard directly from God. In my undergraduate days at a small Christian college, a group of us met with the president to protest the recent expulsion of a classmate because his hair was too long. In mid-sentence, the president interrupted me to call us to prayer. In his prayer, he asked God to open our minds and hearts to see things his way, the way ordained by God. And then he said, "Thanks for coming to me to share your concerns. My door is always open."

I hesitate also because others who want such an experience have not had one. A friend of mine went to Bible camp as a young adolescent. In camp, they prayed for the outpouring of the Holy Spirit and the gift of speaking in tongues. They prayed at night watch services around a campfire. They prayed on a hillside at morning watch as the sun came up. They prayed at revival services during the day when visiting preachers called them to Christ and to receive the Holy Spirit's gift of tongues as confirmation of their faith. One by one his friends felt the rush of the Spirit. They spoke in tongues and were baptized. My friend prayed and prayed, but he never felt anything. He never spoke in tongues. He concluded that God was not interested in him, which in turn hardened him toward God. It took forty years, but finally the Holy Spirit broke through his defenses and overwhelmed him with God's love. He realized finally that Jesus' death and resurrection were sufficient for him. A new man was born the day that good news got through.

We hesitate to speak of spiritual experiences because often they are ordinary and seem unremarkable, even banal. However, that is the nature of the means of grace—ordinary bread, wine, and water. Ordinary words bear to us the Word, Jesus, Son of God and Son of Man, who is ordinary flesh and blood. Common words formulate the good news and convey to us not words about Jesus, but Jesus himself.

We recoil from a treacly piety we sense in those who claim close encounters with God. Someone told me, "I was late getting to the hospital. The streets were crowded with cars. I prayed to God for a parking spot. Someone pulled out of a spot not three car lengths in front of me. With a prayer of thanks and praise I pulled into the place meant for me." I think of that on busy days when visiting the hospital and what I hear from God is, "What makes you so special? Maybe the people in these spots have greater need of them than do you. Drive on a couple of blocks. You will find an open spot. The exercise will do you good." That answer from God is no less worthy of a prayer of thanks and praise.

I hesitate to speak of spiritual experiences because I lack the vocabulary. The dominant vocabulary for encountering our world is that of scientific methodology. Seeing is believing. If others cannot duplicate your results, they are not valid. An Old Testament professor faced a skeptic's question regarding all the strange and wondrous things we read in the Bible. The teacher answered that nothing happened back then that does not happen now. So, if Moses parted the Red Sea and Elisha parted the Jordan River, and those things do not happen today, we must conclude that both of these accounts are legends. If we take Scripture at face value, God spoke to the prophets of old as clearly as we speak to one another on the telephone. If we do not hear God's voice in this manner today, they did not hear it in that manner back then. If seas and rivers do not part now as described in Scripture, they did not part that way for Moses and Elisha—that is, if Moses and Elisha are historical figures. Never did it occur to my professor or to anyone in the class to use this logic to approach this question from the other direction. If it happened back then as described in Scripture, it does happen today in the same manner.

Forwarding the disenchantment program of higher criticism, the professor cited the flood stories common in the ancient literature of other cultures as evidence that the biblical account is not historic. One student suggested that the pervasiveness of the story in other cultures, not only of the ancient Near East, but worldwide, is evidence that such a flood did happen. He went to great lengths to protect the inerrancy of Scripture. He said that all these strange and wondrous things in the Scripture happened as narrated. And now we have the Bible, and we do not need such firsthand revelations any longer. The Bible is our firsthand revelation.

The professor followed the rules of higher criticism for the so-called scientific study of Scripture. His student held the inerrancy of Scripture as sacrosanct and would twist himself this way and that in order to explain how a six-day creation squares with reason. They both spoke the language of science and assumed that that language is the only vocabulary we have. They are what I have called modern-day flat-earthers. Originally, the term applied to those who resisted the claims of science that the earth is round and revolves around the sun. They resisted the conclusions of science because their conceptual field did not include scientific methodology. What was visible to the naked eye and, in many cases, evidence from the Bible, determined their conceptual field. According to what is visible to the naked eye, the earth is flat; the sun, moon, and stars revolve around it. According to Scripture, "Joshua spoke to the Lord; and he said in the sight of Israel, 'Sun, stand still at Gibeon, and Moon, in the valley of Aijalon.' And the sun stood still, and the moon stopped" (Josh 10:12–13). Scripture teaches that the earth and humankind are the crown of God's creation. It follows that all revolves around the earth. God commanded the sun, not the earth, to stand still to give Joshua daylight to pursue Israel's enemies. Scientific methodology binds the conceptual field of those on the other side of the coin.

The physicist Niels Bohr is called the father of quantum mechanics. He claimed an early epiphany from observing the family fish pond. He realized that the fish did not know he was observing them.

> The fish were unaware of any reality outside the pond . . . Even when it rained, the fish saw this not as an event from the outside but only as ripples and splashes enclosed in their environment. Bohr wondered if humans were like the fish in this regard, being acted on in multiple dimensions of reality but aware of only our limited frame of reference.[8]

8. Long, *Testimony*, 42.

For readers such as myself, Bohr's account is a parable about the limitations of our knowledge and an argument in favor of what is real but beyond our ability to weigh and measure. This, however, is not the lesson Bohr received from his epiphany. For example, in the preface to a collection of lectures, he claims that the development of modern atomic physics provides the framework for establishing facts in other disciplines.[9] The lectures include a 1932 address to the International Congress on Light Therapy and one in 1939 to the International Congress of Anthropological and Ethnological Sciences. One may be surprised to find a master of the hard sciences deliver lectures to practitioners of what often are called the soft sciences. Bohr never spoke down to the audiences of these seven lectures. He was a proponent of the unity of knowledge, but it would be knowledge gained "under reproducible and communicable conditions."[10] Toward the close of his lecture to the Congress on Light Therapy, he said, "I should like to emphasize that considerations of the kind here mentioned are entirely opposed to any attempt of seeking new possibilities for a spiritual influence."[11] Bohr acknowledged the need to accommodate differing fields of inquiry while recognizing epistemological commonalities. He said, "We have to do with a rational development of our means of classifying and comprehending new experience." What we are about is "far from containing any mysticism contrary to the spirit of science."[12]

In my estimation, Bohr would only increase the size of the fish pond. In 1901–1902, thirty years prior to the first lecture in Bohr's collection, William James, a Harvard psychologist and philosopher, delivered the Gifford Lectures, twenty addresses on natural religion at the University of Edinburgh in Scotland. He wrote, "It is as if there were in the human consciousness a *sense of reality, a feeling of objective presence, a perception* of what we may call '*something there*,' more deep and more general than any of

9. Bohr, *Atomic Physics*, v.

10. Bohr, *Atomic Physics*, 26.

11. Bohr, *Atomic Physics*, 11.

12. Bohr, *Atomic Physics*, 26–27.

the special and particular 'senses' by which the current psychology supposes existent realities to be originally revealed."[13]

More than a century later, James Smith acknowledges that "the existential world is flat."[14] He writes, "Employing a kind of intellectual colonialism, new atheist cartographers rename entire regions of our experience and annex them to natural science and empirical explanation, flattening the world by disenchantment."[15] Smith serves as interpreter, apologist, and critic of Charles Taylor's cultural anthropology *A Secular Age*. Following Taylor, Smith refers to a "'Jamesian Open Space' where we recognize the contestability of our *take* on things."[16] Those who consider their take on transcendence to be "just the way things are" are fundamentalists, secular fundamentalists on the one hand and religious fundamentalists on the other.[17] Religious fundamentalist maps are flattened by a disenchantment similar to that of their secular kin. A professor at a conservative Christian college told his class they could believe Jonah was swallowed by a big fish because in 1898 a Japanese fisherman fell off his boat and was swallowed by a whale. The whale spat him up, and he lived to tell about it. He noted that the account was available in the newspapers, although he failed to provide a bibliographic reference.

Marilynne Robinson seems to have these ideas in mind when she writes, "[E]ven theology has embraced impoverishment, often under the name of secularism, in order to blend more thoroughly into a disheartened cultural landscape."[18]

The first professor's higher criticism ran aground on the shoals of irrelevance. The student and the second professor's contortions are practiced yet in many expressions of Christ's church. Those contortions lead people out of the church and out of the faith when they can no longer believe that dinosaurs and humans

13. James, *Varieties of Religious Experience*, 59.

14. Smith, *How (Not) To Be Secular*, viii.

15. Smith, *How (Not) To Be Secular*, 2.

16. Smith, *How (Not) To Be Secular*, 94.

17. Smith, *How (Not) To Be Secular*, 95.

18. Robinson, *Absence of Mind*, 35.

walked the earth at the same time and the earth is five-thousand-or-so years old. The evidence to the contrary is overwhelming.

Make no mistake. I highly value science. I simply don't want it to be the only language I speak. I want to be bilingual. I want also to speak the language of our Scriptures, the language of spiritual experiences. Additionally, I need an alternative community in which people speak the language of faith. The church is the alternative community for learning, speaking, and propagating that language. I refer the reader back to chapter 2 and to the hermeneutic for hearing and receiving God's revelation from the pages of Scripture. In the resurrection narratives, we hear the evangelists, Matthew, Mark, Luke, and John struggle with the limitations of our language to describe what happens outside the boundaries of the territory in which our language developed. Language is bounded as we are by time, birth, and death. In the visions of Isaiah 25 and Revelation, in the constitution for the kingdom of God in Matthew 5–7 (indeed, throughout Scripture), we encounter a new language, ethos, and way of living that does not square with the old order. The grave draws the boundary lines of the old order. No boundaries or walls are evident in the new life we have in Christ.

Even Paul spoke reluctantly about his own spiritual experiences (2 Cor 12:1–10; cf. Gal 1:15–16). When he does so, he tells it in the third person, as though to distance himself from it. He had trouble describing it. Twice he says, "I do not know; God knows" as he searches for the right words. The reason Paul did not talk about his experiences was not because he lived in an era in which people did not talk about such things. On the contrary, in the Corinthian congregation in particular, it was almost the only thing people talked about. The people in the church in Corinth were all in the gifted program. They were not intellectually gifted or financially gifted, or gifted in sports. Or, if some of them were, these were not the gifts that counted in the first church of Corinth. Spiritual gifts were what they were after, and they claimed to have them. Paul does not argue with them on that point. What Paul took issue with was how these gifts were being used in the community. People used them to promote themselves or their group. They became a source of bragging rights, and then consequently division in the community. That is our old sinful nature at work. We take the gifts God has given us and use them to promote ourselves and to demote others, and that can get ugly, even in the church. To Paul's dismay, he saw the gospel being buried under all this promotion of spiritual gifts. Somewhere in the mix they forgot all about Jesus being crucified and raised.

A man I know was in a county jail waiting to be arraigned on charges brought against him. During this time, a number of pastors visited. Typically, visitors talk with prisoners in what they call the cages, squatting on little stools, looking at one another through scratched Plexiglas and straining to hear each other through a pegboard opening. It is designed so that nothing can be passed through, but the design makes it hard for words to pass through too.

One of the pastors who visited the incarcerated man was unknown to him, and he had no idea how this pastor even learned about him. The pastor posed as an attorney. That dodge gave him the privilege of meeting with him in a room. The pastor asked the prisoner if he spoke in tongues, advising him that if he did not speak in tongues, then he was not a real Christian. He then proceeded to pray in tongues, and told the prisoner to ask God for the gift of tongues. Then he went on his way. The pastor may have meant well, but his visit amounted to a stickup. He attempted to rob the prisoner of the comfort of his faith. Effectively, his message was that Jesus' death and resurrection are not enough. We also have to speak in tongues.

Paul cherished his experience. He usually kept it to himself, but not this time. Some interlopers at the church were boasting of their spiritual experiences and Paul's lack of them as evidence of their credentials to lead and the need for Paul to head on down the road. Paul listed out his spiritual experience to say, in effect, "This one tops all of yours. If I was to boast about such a thing I could." "But I refrain from it, so that no one may think better of me than what is seen in me or heard from me" (2 Cor 12:6). Did you catch the comment aimed at the interlopers? What people saw in them was self-promotion. What they saw in Paul was a life centered around the gospel. What they heard was that Christ was crucified and raised for the forgiveness of our sins, a balm to troubled consciences and a Word that transforms our lives from boasting to service.

If Paul were to boast, he would boast only in his own weaknesses. And he certainly had them. Don't we all? After recounting such a remarkable spiritual high, Paul wrote, "Therefore to keep me from being too elated, a thorn was given me in the flesh, a messenger of Satan to torment me, to keep me from being too elated" (2 Cor 12:7). This image of a splinter in his finger is totally inadequate. What the text describes is a distracting annoyance. What Paul described was something much more ominous. The word translated "thorn" was, in fact, a pointed stake planted in the ground as the ancient version of a landmine. They didn't explode, but if a defensive perimeter had enough of these concealed in dugout areas, significant damage could be done to advancing foes, who fell and impaled themselves on these stakes.[19] Paul wrote, "Such a stake impaled my flesh, a messenger of Satan to cause me agony."

The stake may be a messenger from Satan, but God is in no way threatened. God is in charge. In Paul's view, we are the battleground over which the struggle is waged. The reign of God advances. The old dispensation digs in and sets up its defenses. This selfish bent was clearly on display in the church in Corinth as groups vied with one another for dominance.

Paul wrote, "Three times I appealed to the Lord about this, that it would leave me." We don't know what it was, and there is no sense speculating about it. But the very fact that we don't know what it was makes it easier for us to see ourselves in Paul: the thorn in our flesh, the stake impaling us.

The answer Paul received from God, as well as the answer we might receive from God, whether we are healed of our affliction or not, is "My grace is sufficient for you." The means of grace, the vehicles, the ways God supplies us with such grace, are God's Word and the sacraments. In ordinary words, Jesus Christ (the Word of

19. Sampley, "Second Letter to the Corinthians," 165.

God) walks among us. Baptism's water is objective evidence that the Spirit of God dwells in us. God promises us it is so. If we ever doubt the Spirit's presence in our lives, we have only to plunge our hand into that water. In the Lord's Supper, the body and blood of the risen Christ feeds us body and soul and gives us a foretaste of our eternal communion with the risen Christ. Luther emphasized the importance of the conversation and consolation of the people of God. That gives us a glimpse of our eternal communion with all the saints of God. "My grace is sufficient for you," says the Lord. God added, "My power is made perfect in your weakness." Cling to the promises: His grace is sufficient for you, and his power is made perfect in your weakness.

Despite our reluctance to speak of it, we do experience God in the course of our daily lives. Talking about such experiences with the same humility of Paul, we give others courage to speak of their own encounters with God. We learn and practice the vocabulary of God's realm.

Many of our encounters with God are ordinary. If we told others about them, they would sound petty. Such encounters offer assurance, and sometimes criticism. At one point, when I was in college, I found myself at the end of a long relationship that had been a source of great joy and great sadness. I dreamt of a young woman, different from the lost love. I did not see the source of the words I heard, but I clearly heard, *Do not be anxious. There is another intended for you. I promise.* I woke at peace.

Years later, in much different circumstances, with a spouse and two children, I appeared on my day off at the local big-box hardware store purchasing supplies for the backyard pool, which, once again, was turning green. My frustration showed. The cashier looked me over, studied what I was purchasing, and commented, "Let's see. You have a swimming pool. It is sunny and 80 degrees. And you're not happy." That forced a smile out of me. I said to her, "You got me." Angel means messenger. Certainly, she was God's messenger to me that day, bearing God's criticism of me that led me to repent. My friend had a similar experience. He told me, "It was not a good day. I had a funeral and was on my way from the cemetery back to church when I stopped in the local fast-food place for some comfort food: a bag of fries and a Coke. I sat at a table eating when I noticed a large black man approaching. I had my clerical collar on. I calculated what I had in my wallet and what I was prepared to give him. He slid into the seat opposite me. He said, 'Do you believe what you preach?' I said, 'On my good days, yes, I believe. On bad days, not so much.' He responded, 'I thought so,' got up, and left."

One person in a church I served told the mid-week Bible study about an experience he had in church. He always came early. He sat in his customary place in the pew. He said it was a good time for meditation. This particular Sunday, he was musing over the death of a friend's wife. Their friendship reached back to college. Her death had been a terrible blow to his friend. Suddenly, out of nowhere but as clear as the transfiguration, he saw her on the stairway into heaven. "It's all right," she said to him. "It's all right." He described it as a conscious dream. He said it was spooky and reassuring at the same time.

Thomas Long, a theologian I greatly respect, related to a conference audience what a woman told him after church one Sunday.

> My husband was dying of cancer. He was in the last hours of his life. The children and I were all there around his bed. He was struggling and I knew what was going on. He had always provided for us, always been the caretaker. I took his face in my hands and I said, "You old redhead. I have loved you since high school and I'm never going to stop loving you. But if you need to go, go. God has always taken care of us and always will. If you are worried about us, send a little red bird once in a while." It wasn't long and he died. We made arrangements with the funeral home, signed what we needed to sign at the hospital. We went home and sat in the family room talking, crying and laughing, remembering him and telling stories about him. A red bird came to the window, sat on the sill, and stayed there for forty-five minutes.

Long said, "There was a time I would have said, 'Bad theology. Sentimental piety.' But now I've come to realize that there is more mystery, wonder, and grace, more God in the world than the little tweezers of my theology can hold."

In Reynolds Price's story "The Foreseeable Future," Whitley Wade was gravely wounded on World War II's D-Day, a quart of his blood and pulverized bone laid down in a green French pasture. The medics thought he was dead and took credit for bringing him back to life, at least as far back as medics can. Now he is back home, back to his family, back at work, but far from back to life, and contemplating ending it all.[20]

While traveling for his job as an insurance claims adjustor, he sits in a "Thanksgiving for Victory" worship service and studies a stained-glass window, consisting of

> a risen Christ stepping out of the tomb. Christ's hips were hardly covered with rags; his palms were outward, displaying their ruin. His side was bleeding and his lips were very nearly smiling. It came as a shock to Whit— that threat of a smile, the first he'd seen in a hundred pictures of this ferocious moment.[21]

Later, stopped on the side of the road to read the map directing him to the next customer, he feels the Spirit wrapping itself around the wound in his chest. "Whit laughed in his heart, his whole new mind . . . He tried to look round, his eyes stayed shut, but he thought he was smiling."[22] When he is back home, he realizes, "The actual world had called him back—people, objects and the thing he prayed to—and now he'd obeyed."[23] In the presence of his wife, he addresses his daughter: "You and your mother are where I've landed. For now at least, the foreseeable future, this May the 11th, 1945. I enjoy the view of both you ladies and the world behind you. May you bypass places that steal your soul. May you find your own home base like me."[24]

20. Price, "Foreseeable Future," 69.

21. Price, "Foreseeable Future," 125.

22. Price, "Foreseeable Future," 183.

23. Price, "Foreseeable Future," 192.

24. Price, "Foreseeable Future," 203.

All fiction is autobiography to some extent. In Price's case, I call it autozoegraphy, *zoe* being the New Testament word for eternal life. He wrote at length about his experiences in a book titled *A Whole New Life: An Illness and a Healing*. He tells his readers, "This is a book about a mid-life collision with cancer and paralysis, a collision I've survived for ten years and counting...

"I've ... worked to show not only the weight of the ordeal but the luck I found right through it—in friends and kin, in medical care (though with daunting exceptions), in my two kinds of work [teaching and writing], and in the now appalling, now astonishing grace of God."[25] He describes his vision of joining Jesus and his disciples on the shore of Galilee. He saw himself baptized by Jesus in its waters, sins forgiven, and healing promised.[26]

It did not take long for Price to experience the effects of treatment. The longer he felt the side effects of treatment, the longer the distance between the present and his vision, and the dimming prognosis for the future turned his experience at the Sea of Galilee into what he called a suspicious assurance. At this crucial time, a minister visited bearing the Lord's Supper. He writes, "[A]s intensely as any mystic, in the eating that one morning, I experienced again the almost overwhelming force" giving him the courage to carry on.[27]

In pedestrian circumstances, Mr. Ives received assurances that all was well with the world. The murder of his son undermined these certainties. He mourned along with his wife and many others who loved the young man. Ives's mourning increased over the years. Stigmata covered his body in the form of hives, which he scratched in his sleep until they bled. Then he had a dream in which his son appeared to him, middle-aged, dressed in priestly robes, wading in the water. His son took him by the hand and led him into the pond. His son said to him, "Pop, why do you keep doing this to yourself?" Then his son poured water over him and washed him before disappearing from sight. When Ives woke up

25. Price, *Whole New Life*, vii–viii.
26. Price, *Whole New Life*, 42–43.
27. Price, *Whole New Life*, 81–82.

in the morning, he looked in the mirror and saw that his skin was smooth and the scabby wounds were gone.[28]

When we consider the mayhem in the world, we have a sense that mayhem is not the way the world is supposed to be. Why not? It is the way it has always been. War and hunger are history's constants. Sickness and disease continue to threaten. The strongest have always ruled. The weak have always been exploited. Might makes right. Life is not fair. Power corrupts. One law of science is that an action causes an equal and opposite reaction. In social science, the law is that any negative or harmful action causes an opposite and *greater* reaction. Joseph Conrad sails us up an African river into the jungle's heart of darkness, only to explore for us the human heart of darkness. Evidence would say this is the way we are, the way the world has always been, is now, and always will be. From where do we get the understanding that these things are not the way life will always be, that there is a new day coming and already at hand? I propose that our spiritual experiences provide assurance for us of what Scripture proclaims. God is in charge. The future God intends for us is good. The power of evil is broken. Christ has died. Christ is risen. Christ will come again. We see evidence of God in current events, in the minutiae of our lives and the banal, and in the promise by which we live.

---

28. Hijuelos, *Mr. Ives' Christmas*, 237–38.

Chapter 5

Eucharistic Living
In Six/Quarter Time

In the first chapter, I stated that my aim for this final chapter was to describe how God and God's reign are present to us, manifest in us, and visible through us as we live in response to the good future revealed to us in the face of Jesus Christ. I call this eucharistic living. Eucharist comes to us from the Greek word for what Jesus did when he took the bread in his hands: he gave thanks. The word is bound up with everything the night, his actions, and his words portend.

> On the night in which he was betrayed, he took the bread, gave thanks, broke it, and gave it to his disciples saying, "Take and eat. This is my body given for you. Do this in remembrance of me." Again, after supper he took the cup, gave thanks, and gave it to them saying, "This cup is the new covenant in my blood, shed for you and for all people for the forgiveness of sin. Do this in remembrance of me." (1 Cor 11:23–25)

These are ancient words. Paul handed them on to the church in Corinth as they had been handed on to him.

John the Evangelist layers an interpretive scene on top of this one. On the night of his betrayal, Jesus knew that all things had been handed over to him. In response to this, he wrapped a towel around his waist, took a basin of water, and knelt to wash his disciples' feet, even the feet of Judas. Walter Bouman writes, "True spiritual priesthood means giving yourself to God for your neighbor's sake, not giving yourselves to your neighbor for God's sake."[1] Knowing that all things had been handed over to him, he knelt to serve. John provides for us an insight into the meaning of Eucharist and eucharistic living. All things have been handed over to us who are in Christ. We turn a changed people. We turn to serve.

Eucharistic living flows out of the pattern we witness at the offertory. Bouman points out that

> Mass means mission. It comes from the final words of the liturgy, "*Ito, missa est,*" "Go, it is the sending!" The sacrament was given to us as a meal, the "feast of victory for our God." The meal was given to us so that we would eat and drink and be sent into the world as the body of Christ, set free to give ourselves for the life of the world.[2]

I did not understand this until I was in seminary, standing in my "fieldwork parish," a little congregation on life support from the judicatory, and saw Pastor H. undo the twist-tie around the package of Wonder Bread and pull out two slices as he prepared to lead the offertory prayer. The ushers had presented the offering plates. Not much in those. The ushers also brought up the wine for communion. On the heels of the ushers, members of the congregation slid out of the pews, joining the offertory procession, and bringing to the altar a bounty of canned goods, bread, and other staple food items. After church, these were taken downstairs to stock the food pantry the congregation sponsored for the neighborhood. However, at the moment, they were part of the offering, and demonstrated to me the connection between offering and Eucharist, as well as the further

1. Bouman, *We Believe*, 131.
2. Bouman, *We Believe*, 115–16.

connection between Eucharist and the church's ministry. Pastor H. always found a loaf of Wonder Bread in the offering, from which he took several slices for the Lord's Supper. I was naïve enough to think that it was by chance that a loaf of Wonder Bread was always present. Twenty-five years later, I reconnected with a member of the congregation and related this memory to him. He said, "Oh yes, I always made sure Pastor H. had a loaf of Wonder Bread for communion."

God regifts our offerings. He gives them back to us for our sake and for the sake of the world. We bring our offerings of bread and wine on Sunday morning. God accepts our offerings, blesses them, and gives them back to us as the means of grace. In, with, and under these elements of bread and wine are the body and blood of Christ, the very means by which God has redeemed us. We bring our offerings of money. In the case of my fieldwork church, we also brought up our gifts of canned goods. God takes what we offer, blesses it, and gives it back into our hands, multiplied for ministry in our community and around the world. We bring our offerings of praise and thanksgiving. God delights in our sacrifice of praise and returns it to us for lives that are eucharistic.

The hymn text "Savior of the Nations Come" is attributed to Saint Ambrose, who lived in the fourth century. It captures the trajectory of what the Eucharist proclaims and the story of which we become a part as we participate in the meal. Stanzas 4–6 proclaim,

> God the Father is his source,
> Back to God he runs his course;
> Down to death and hell descends,
> God's high throne he reascends.
>
> He leaves heaven to return;
> Trav'ling where dull hellfires burn;
> Riding out, returning home
> As the Savior who has come.
>
> God the Father's precious Son
> Girds himself in flesh to run
> For the trophies of our souls,
> Longer than this round earth rolls.[3]

---

3. Ambrose, "Savior of the Nations, Come," 28.

In this hymn, the atonement is proclaimed as it is in the Lord's Supper, as God's resolve to restore us to himself. Here we do not meet a Heavenly Father who must extract his pound of flesh from someone for offenses given. Eucharist enacts atonement as participation in the Triune God. As we in faith eat and drink the body and blood of Christ, we are drawn into the divine life. Participation in the Triune God "does not leave the one upon whom the spirit rests unchanged," writes Gregory Walter. "This resting is a dwelling, an opening that is given to unblock the closed possibilities of the past and to allow individuals and communities to act in novel ways and to risk what seems impossible. This means that the promise is a gift to another; it gives the gift of action, of possibility to another, and so opens up a field of action, the field of love."[4]

Lutherans are careful to say we are not reconciled to God by our good works, but by faith in Jesus Christ. By faith we cling to God's promise; by faith we abide in Christ. Moreover, we say faith is not something we achieve, but the free gift of God's Holy Spirit. The Holy Spirit calls, gathers, enlightens, and regenerates us through the gospel. The gospel is God's promise that our sins are forgiven, we are reconciled with God, and are heirs of eternal life by Jesus' death and resurrection for us. We also say that because of this faith we do good works and keep the law of God.[5] The law demands hearts that are obedient to God. The law can and does coerce our behavior, but it cannot touch our hearts. A wide range of evidence backs up this assertion, but let this one prosaic example suffice.

Our son attended a Jesuit high school across town from where we lived at the time. Prior to his junior year, we purchased a used car for him. It was a birthday present that came with a string attached. He had to agree to drive a carpool for younger Jesuit students in our vicinity for one year. The going rate was ten dollars per week. Three carpoolers provided him with gas money and lessened the transfer from my wallet to his. He called them "my

---

4. Walter, *Being Promised*, 58.
5. Kolb and Wengert, *Book of Concord*, 167.

freshmen." One of these was Leonard Klein (not his real name). When our son arrived at Leonard's house on the second day of school, Mr. Klein came out with his son. Mr. Klein was a large man, over six feet five inches, with the girth of Goliath. He leaned into the open driver's side window. Resting his weight on the door frame, he drove the little Honda to its knees. He said to our son, "The route you drove to school yesterday is just fine except for that last turn. It is a dangerous intersection. I want you to go one more block to the stoplight. It will be safer to make the left turn from there."

Our son knew there was one of two ways Mr. Klein knew the route he drove. Either Mr. Klein's son told his father or Mr. Klein had followed him on the first day of school. One look in the rearview mirror at the mortified expression on the face of young Klein and he knew which it was. That morning our son watched for Mr. Klein and sure enough spotted him several car lengths back. He took the route as directed.

Months later we attended a social gathering of parents at the school. I talked with Mrs. Klein. I joked (I thought) with her about the time her husband followed our son to school. I said, "I can just see him trailing Leonard on his first date."

She said, "How did you hear about that?"

"I didn't," I said. "I was just joking."

"Well, he did. We let Leonard go on a double date with a friend of his who is old enough to drive. My husband followed them to the restaurant where they went before a dance at school. He waited in the parking lot at school and followed them home when the dance was over."

Mr. Klein established rules and enforced them. Leonard was an obedient son. Following graduation from high school, Leonard went away to college. However, by all accounts, he felt as though he had been set free. He lived with abandon in his newfound freedom. He flunked out. After one semester he was back home.

The law can coerce our behavior, but it cannot change our hearts. The gospel can. God promises that by Jesus' death and resurrection for us our sins are forgiven, we are reconciled to God,

and are heirs now of eternal life. This gospel comforts us and regenerates our hearts for obedience to God.

We do good works because we are regenerated, reborn, by
faith in Jesus. It would be as straightforward as it sounds were it
not for the old Adam and Eve being alive and well in us, no matter how often we drown them by repentance. We Lutherans are
also fond of saying we are at the same time saint and sinner, *simul
justus et peccator*, if you are attracted by the Latin. It is not that
we are sometimes one and sometimes the other, but both at the
same time and all the time. There is no time we are not those who
are baptized into Christ Jesus. When God looks at us, he sees his
Son. There is also no time when the devil is not at work in the old
sinner that we are, flexing its muscle and ready to compromise the
most noble thing we do. Nevertheless, there is something different about the way we live because we live in Christ. Forgiven, we
forgive. Recipients of God's mercy, we become mercy managers
on behalf of others. Such living comes naturally to the regenerated
child of God. It does not come naturally to the old Adam and Eve.
Both of these occupy the same territory: us. They occupy two different atmospheres. When Jesus calls the disciples to follow him
and become fishers for people, he uses a violent image. Fishing is
violent. Those who fish by pole or net drag their prey from a wa-
tery environment, where they are at home, and pull them into the
air, where they will die. By God's grace, the Spirit drags us from a
deadly environment where we are very much at home into the water where we die with Christ. We rise from the water, reborn to live
our lives wet, as it were. We are never quite at home in a poisoned
atmosphere we know is passing away. Using another metaphor, the
regenerated live in six-four time, out of step with the old order's
four-four time signature.

The world out there marks off the year with four seasons.
We do as well, inasmuch as we are a part of that world. The four
seasons beat out the rhythm of the year and the rhythm of our
lives in four-four time: winter, spring, summer, fall, winter, spring,
summer, fall. It is a rhythm for marching, a martial beat. And
where does such a year begin? With the greening of spring, the

lengthening of daylight from December 21, or the beginning of winter on January 1? It has neither beginning nor ending, it seems. Time is simply one endless repetition, one long march of winter, spring, summer, fall, until it all falls apart, as the physicists say it must in a big implosion to match the big bang.

As God's people, as those who are a part of Christ, we have come to mark time differently. We mark time not according to the cycle of the sun, but according to the life cycle of Jesus Christ, the Son of God. We mark off the year in six-four time: Advent, Christmas, Epiphany, Lent, Easter, Pentecost. You cannot march to such a beat, but you might hear in the rhythm what you could do with it: Advent, Christmas, Epiphany, Lent, Easter, Pentecost, Advent, Christmas, Epiphany, Lent, Easter, Pentecost. You could waltz to it. It is a dance rhythm. I find that delightful. But there is an inherent problem here for us inasmuch as we live in the world. Imagine marching up Chicago's State Street, New York's Fifth Avenue, or Any Town's Main Street for the Thanksgiving Day Parade. The bands are all playing marching tunes, all in step, moving in four-four time. But here we come, listening to a different beat, waltzing up the avenue. I imagine the Magi waltzing through the wilderness and into Herod's palace. It is true that we fall out of the waltz step once in a while because that other music around us is so strong. But then we hear the six-four rhythm again in sacrament and sacred story. Those around us are there to help. They are our dance partners in the community of faith. They say, "Don't you feel the beat? Tune out those other rhythms. Get back in step."

The year in six-four time has a definite beginning: Advent. You can tell it is Advent when it is blue in church. Wearing green during Advent would be as big a fashion faux pas as wearing yellow seersucker in winter. We begin the year not with resolutions or talk of a new beginning. Here in six-four time we begin the year by talking about endings. So in Advent not only do we wear blue, but we also sing the blues. The blues are about endings. Bobby Blue Bland sings, "Without a warning, you broke my heart. You took it, shook it; you tore it apart. You left me sitting in the dark crying. You said your love for me was dying." The blues are about endings.

Consider this Old Testament precursor to the Gospel reading. Isaiah sings the blues: "See the day of the Lord comes, cruel, with wrath and fierce anger, to make the earth a desolation, and to destroy its sinners from it. For the stars of the heavens and their constellations will not give their light; the sun will be dark at its rising and the moon will not shed its light . . . I will make mortals more rare than fine gold" (13:9–12a). Those are the blues. "Without a warning you broke my heart. You took it, shook it; you tore it apart. You left me sitting in the dark crying. You said your love for me was dying." Would that be God or us doing the singing?

In either case the blues, including the Advent Blues, are about endings, an ending that is a big implosion to match the big bang by which it all began. It is a day of reckoning when the Son of Man comes with the clouds to settle all accounts. It is a day such as the day would be if all the credit offers we've taken were to come due on the same day. I'm thinking of the ones advertised on TV. Buy rooms full of furniture, no payments until June of 2021. Throw in some new carpet and window treatments. Buy now, pay later. Low-interest student loan. Repayment deferred until you get that big paying job after graduation. A zero-interest new car loan. There will never be a deal like this again. It's a steal. You need it now. I feel a blues song coming on. "I took it on credit. I lived without a care. I had coins in my pocket, money to spare. But now all those loans have come due. What am I gonna do?" So will be the day of reckoning when the Son of Man comes with the clouds. What are we gonna do?

But wait a minute now. There is something wrong here. This whole analogy is built on the notion that it is God who extends us credit. I have no doubt that we are indebted to God, but I don't think it's because he's given us credit for sinning. Credit is essentially what faith is. The Latin word is *credo*. It means *I believe*. From *credo* we get both creed and credit. Someone extends credit to us based on their faith in us that we will pay up. Based on Jesus' initial public offering of resurrection, as someone has called it, we've put our faith in him. We have his word that he will make good on his promise. God gives us his Holy Spirit as what Paul refers to as the first installment on what is promised (2 Cor 1:22; 5:5). God knows our willingness to extend credit might depend on something tangible, so he gives us baptism and Eucharist as surety, promissory notes. Paul talks about them as down payments, some earnest money that he will fulfill his promise. So when this Son of Man comes with the clouds, stand up, lift up your heads, for your redemption is at hand. It is a joyous event for us his creditor-believers. He has made a lot of promises, and expensive ones at that. When he comes with the clouds at the end of history for a day of reckoning, he comes to pay out. With his lavish payout, we are more than redeemed from our own debts. The Advent Blues are about endings and also about hope. Bobby Bland is hopeful. "Turn on your light," he pleads. "Turn on your love light. Let it shine on me. Let it shine, shine, shine." When the Son of Man comes with the clouds, stand up, lift up your heads, for your redemption is at hand (Matt 25).

On that day, we either rise from the grave or push open our screen door and step out on our front porch to meet him, depending on what time of year he makes his Advent. That we begin a new year talking about endings is a clue as to our attitude towards the end, that we are looking at an ending that is a new beginning. In this new creation, all our losses are made good. It may be the loss of those we love, the loss that comes with illness, or the time that is closing in on us, about which another bluesman, Bob Seeger, sings in his song "Night Moves."

His song begins with the sort of moves that take place under cover of darkness "in the back seat of his '60 Chevy." They end some thirty years later when a thunderclap woke him from sleep. The thunderclap is the clap of doom. He wonders how far off it is as he starts "humming a song from 1962," and wonders where the years have gone. "When time is closing in, ain't it funny how the night moves?" he sings at the end.

You name what it is behind that empty feeling that comes upon you, that has you singing the blues. In the new creation, all our losses are made good. Oddly enough, our losses often are caused by what we have too much of: smugness, resentment, fear, self-hatred. At the risk of mixing too many metaphors, Jesus' crucifixion, that ending, is the winnowing in which the chaff of our lives is lifted by the harvester's pitchfork so that the wind might blow away the chaff and the grain fall back to the ground to be saved. His crucifixion is the refiner's fire burning away the dross of our lives. His crucifixion is the farmer's harrow breaking up the hard soil of our hearts to make them hospitable places for Jesus. He makes us fitting dance partners, so we follow his lead into the new creation.

In the meantime, Jesus says, "Be on guard so that your hearts are not weighed down with dissipation and drunkenness . . . Be alert, pray that you might stand before me" (Luke 21:34). If he is our righteousness (and he is), then we will stand before him. Isn't this advice that Jesus gives an admonition to live according to six-four time now? The world around might regard us as drunk, the way they did the disciples at the first Pentecost. But we know what really weighs us down: that old four-four time. So be on your guard, be alert, pray, be attentive to the music of the new creation, those Advent Blues of endings and the hope of new beginnings. Practice the rhythm we hear in sacred story, baptism, and Eucharist. Stick with your dance partners in the community of faith. And do your part to help one another stay in step with the new creation dance. Dance in the midst of a world bent on other rhythms, mostly of destruction. Show them new possibilities, new creation promise, and lead them to make the investment, extend the credit that is faith in Jesus, who at his advent makes good on all our losses.

The secular age in which we live is a flattened and decolored landscape. The dominant rhythm is provided by the drumbeat of conflict. God draws in the background the contours of a new creation. With bright colors he sketches out a new dimension in which weapons of war become farm implements, the lion and calf lie down together, all tears are wiped away, and death is no more. The cross of Jesus is the starting point for God's new creation work. We take up our cross and follow Jesus. God gives us the eyes to see and the ears to hear the kingdom of God at hand. He calls us to gain our footing in this new dimension so that we might extend the benefits of new life in Christ to all people and all of God's creation.

The Gospels do not end with all loose ends tied up. Life is not like that. From Scripture we do know some things about how God resolves this current order, drawing it into his kingdom. Eucharistic living in six-four time takes its direction from the visions of Daniel and Revelation, the prophets' words, the teachings of Jesus, the apostles' letters, and the example of the saints who have gone before us. We know we are still on the way. Daily we take up our cross, our death, to follow Jesus.

Contrary to the belief of many, God is not absent from us. But God is hidden. The remarkable thing is that God reveals himself by hiding. He chooses only the banal in which to hide his grace. The invisible God irrevocably cloaks himself in Jesus' body, and Jesus reveals God to us. God in Christ hides in the suffering of the cross and signals God's presence to us wherever there is suffering. God is present in the gritty work of reconciliation. The Spirit reveals God as present in the ordinary as we live in ordinary time. God hides in common bread, wine, water, and words. In my experience, when people are asked what they most want to hear from another person, their first answer is "I love you." The second answer is "I forgive you." The third answer is "Come to supper." This latter answer is humorous and is meant to dodge serious consideration of the question. But with the ordinary means at hand, especially as we come into church on a Sunday morning, we hear from God, "I love you; I forgive you; come to my Supper. The table is set."

The hymn "Jesus, Still Lead On," sung to Adam Drese's tune "Seelenbraütigam," is one of the many hymns with a six-four time signature in the hymnals with which I am most familiar. There is no difference in the rhythm between the six-four and three-four time signatures. Composers write six-four time to indicate that the tune is not to be played like a jig. It is to be slower and more deliberate. "Jesus, Still Lead On" sung in this way sums up life in six-four time. It is difficult to be out of step with the old order's four-four rhythm. However, the One who is an expert at six-four time has taken us by the hand.

Jesus, still lead on, till our rest be won;
And, although the way be cheerless,
We will follow, calm and fearless;
Guide us by the hand to the promised land.[6]

---

6. Zinzendorf, "Jesus, Still Lead On," 624.

Discussion Questions

Chapter 1: Prolegomenon

1. The author begins with a story about a church in Tennessee. He concludes by making the point that sometimes the sign (the church) and the thing signified (the kingdom of God) come together "to give visible witness to God's promised new creation." What examples can you cite from congregations and ministries that you know about or have been part of?

2. Citing research from the Church Innovations Institute, the author notes a tendency to talk about what we are doing in ministry while avoiding language about what God is doing. If you can, please tell of some instances in which this was the case, and others in which it was not. Either way, why do you think it was so?

3. The author says "we live in the overlap of two eras: the one in which sin, death, and devil hold sway and the other being the kingdom of God." When asked for his own example, the author said, "Funerals. We process into the church with a dead body behind a cross, an instrument of execution, singing a hymn about resurrection and Christ's triumph over death for us." When and where have you witnessed this overlap?

Chapter 2: The Means of Grace

1. The author claims that in Word and sacraments and their attendants, worship and music, God gives us glimpses of God's kingdom come. Have you experienced such a glimpse of God's kingdom come? What about the worship service gave you that glimpse?

2. The main character in Robert Olen Butler's story "Up by Heart" quotes Scripture in a way that drives people away. When have you experienced Scripture used in such a fashion? When have you heard Scripture used in a way that drew you in?

3. The author said, "In worship we seek to reflect the beauty, grandeur, and grace of God." When in worship have you seen this? Do you have suggestions of ways we might better reflect the beauty grandeur and grace of God in worship?

Chapter 3: The Ministry of Reconciliation

1. The author quotes Paul in 2 Corinthians 5:16–19 saying God "has given us the ministry of reconciliation; that is, in Christ God was reconciling the world to himself." Can you tell a story from your experience of God's reconciling work? How does a local example affect the world?

2. The author's examples all involve people of faith. Have you seen ways God works reconciliation in the world apart from the church of Christ? Where have you seen such examples?

3. Can you tell stories of reconciliation you know about or have been part of in your family, church, or place of employment?

4. Has your faith community experienced a divide between those who want to welcome LGBTQ people into the congregation and those who do not? If so, how have you (or could you) navigate that divide?

Chapter 4: Spiritual Experiences

1. The author calls the opening narrative "a profound spiritual experience." Have you had a profound spiritual experience?

2. The author describes in some detail the reasons people hesitate to admit to spiritual experiences. Share your reactions to the reasons he cites. Are there additional explanations of why people might stay silent?

3. How can you help people recognize and talk about their spiritual experiences?

Chapter 5: Eucharistic Living: In Six/Quarter Time

1. After reading this chapter, how would you define Eucharistic Living?

2. The author claims the ministry of the people of God flows from the Lord's Supper. Think of the ministries of your congregation and those in which you are involved. How do they connect with Holy Communion?

3. Jesus said, "You will know the truth and the truth will make you free." Flannery O'Connor said the truth will make you odd. What images does the author use to describe the experience of being a Christian in this world? Which of those images do you relate to? Which others would you add?

4. Reflect on the author's claim that God reveals Godself to us by hiding. Where in your own life have you experienced God revealed in hiddenness?

Bibliography

Allen, Diogenes. *Spiritual Theology*. Lanham: Cowley, 1997.

————. *Steps Along the Way: A Spiritual Autobiography*. New York: Church Publishing, 2002.

Ambrose. "Savior of the Nations, Come." In *Lutheran Book of Worship*, translated by Martin L. Seltz, 28. Minneapolis: Augsburg, 1978.

Bachfeuer. "Pat Robertson Prayed Hurricane Gloria Away from Virginia Beach in '85." https://www.youtube.com/watch?v=3Uj7Jj4F8vA.

Berger, Peter L. *A Rumor of Angels: Modern Society and Rediscovery of the Supernatural*. Garden City, NY: Doubleday, 1970.

Bodenstab, Eric. "The Actors Are Come Hither." PhD diss., Luther Seminary, 2014.

Bohr, Niels. *Atomic Physics and Human Knowledge*. Mineola, NY: Dover, 2010.

Bouman, Walter R. *We Believe*. Delhi, NY: American Lutheran Publicity Bureau, 1999.

Bragg, Rick. *My Southern Journey: True Stories from the Heart of the South*. New York: Oxmoor, 2015.

Bretscher, Paul G. *The Foolishness of God: A Manual for the Confirmation Instruction of Children, Drawn from the Holy Scriptures according to Luther's Small Catechism*. Valparaiso: Immanuel Curriculum of Immanuel Lutheran Church, 1983.

Butler, Robert Olen. "Up by Heart." In *Had a Good Time: Stories from American Postcards*, 201–27. New York: Grove, 2012.

Hijuelos, Oscar. *Mr. Ives' Christmas*. New York: HarperCollins, 1995.

Hinlicky, Paul R. *Luther vs. Pope Leo: A Conversation in Purgatory*. Nashville: Abingdon, 2017.

James, William. *The Varieties of Religious Experience: A Study in Human Nature*. New York: Vintage, 1990.

Keifert, Patrick. *We Are Here Now: A New Missional Era*. Eagle, ID: Allelon, 2006.

Kolb, Robert, and Timothy J. Wengert, eds. *The Book of Concord*. Minneapolis: Fortress, 2000.

Bibliography

Long, Thomas G. *Testimony: Talking Ourselves into Being Christian*. San Francisco: Jossey-Bass, 2004.

Price, Reynolds. "The Foreseeable Future." In *The Foreseeable Future*, 61–204. New York: Athenum, 1991.

———. *A Whole New Life: An Illness and a Healing*. New York: Athenum, 1994.

RightWingWatchdotorg. "Pat Robertson, in His Own Words, on Running for President." https://www.youtube.com/watch?v=dewVSJoUU18.

Robinson, Marilynne. *Absence of Mind: The Dispelling of Inwardness from the Modern Myth of the Self*. New Haven, CT: Yale University Press, 2010.

Sampley, J. Paul. "Second Letter to the Corinthians." In *The New Interpreter's Bible*, 11:3–180. Nashville: Abingdon, 2000.

Senn, Frank C. *Introduction to Christian Liturgy*. Minneapolis: Fortress, 2012.

Simpson, Gary. "God, Civil Society, and Congregations as Public Moral Companions." In *Testing the Spirits: How Theology Informs the Study of Congregations*, edited by Patrick Keifert, 67–88. Grand Rapids, MI: Eerdmans, 2009.

Smith, James K. A. *How (Not) To Be Secular: Reading Charles Taylor*. Grand Rapids, MI: Eerdmans, 2014.

Walter, Gregory. *Being Promised: Theology, Gift, and Practice*. Grand Rapids, MI: Eerdmans, 2013.

Wilken, Robert Louis. "With Angels and Archangels." In *Pro Ecclesia* 10.4 (202) 460–74.

Zinzendorf, Nicholas Lidwig von. "Jesus Still Lead On." In *Evangelical Lutheran Worship*, translated by Jane L. Borthwick, 624. Minneapolis: Augsburg Fortress, 2006.

CPSIA information can be obtained
at www.ICGtesting.com
Printed in the USA
FSHW011949250919
62403FS